Our Little Piece of Paradise

of

Paradise

Karen Telling

Michael Terence
Publishing

First published in paperback by
Michael Terence Publishing in 2022
www.mtp.agency

ISBN 9781800942998

To all the members of our four-legged family,
past, present and future...

Whether you are with us for hours, days, months or years,
we love you just the same.

Prologue

This book follows on directly from my first Another Day in Paradise, it's probably advisable to read them in sequence.

I didn't intend to write a sequel, but I have received many requests for an update. Initially I thought I would write a short piece about our rescue animals, but bits of us kept creeping in, and eventually I realised I might have enough material for another book after all.

Thank you for reading.

1

September 2004, Barney

We often say we don't know if we bought the house and Barney came free, or vice versa. It always felt as if it was his house before it was ours. We moved in a day after signing the deeds, with help from my mum and dad and friends from the U.K., José and Carol, who happened to be in Portugal staying at their holiday apartment in the Eastern Algarve.

It was such a relief to finally have a home of our own again, and we started to unpack the few boxes that we had trailed from one rental to the other. Barney lay at the bottom of the garden, unsure of what was going on. This was his base, his home territory, and these strangers were invading it. He showed no signs of aggression at all, he didn't even bark, but just watched quietly, at a distance. My mum noticed and went to sit beside him. As she stroked his head she reassured him,

"You don't know it yet, but this is probably the best day of your life and the best thing that could happen to you."

He lay his head on his front paws and watched.

It didn't take long to find a place for everything, for now. There was very little storage, just a few kitchen cupboards and a fridge/freezer that we had bought from Tom, the previous owner, but there was no wardrobe or chest of drawers. Anything that couldn't be stored away was stacked in the room that we planned to turn back into a second bathroom. It was just as well we had brought so few belongings with us. Most importantly our antique bedstead was assembled and made up, then Nick went off to pick up a sofa that we had bought from the furniture shop for whom he did deliveries. The next most important people arrived, the satellite TV installers. We had used the same local company several times already. They had installed a system in our rental apartment, and temporary ones in the two houses we had rented, but now we could have our own choice of TV channels. They set to work with ladders and lengths of cables, Barney gave a sigh and turned his back on the noise and the chaos.

Nick arrived back with the new sofa, we had needed a man with a van after all, and some fresh filled rolls and pastries from the local bakery. Seeing the food made us suddenly ravenous after all the hard work, so Mum and Carol started handing out lunch and drinks to everyone, using whatever random plates and cutlery, mugs and glasses that they could find. We all found somewhere to perch around the garden and stopped for a break. Now, this was more interesting for Barney, his nose twitched at the scent of the ham and cheese, and he moved a little closer. Nick broke off a piece of cheese and held it out.

"Come on Barney, do you like cheese?"

Barney hesitated, looking around at all the expectant faces, then gently took the food from Nick's hand. A piece of ham followed, then more cheese, Barney's tail wagged, and we felt him start to trust us.

The house was now as ready as it could be under the circumstances, so Nick and I headed back to the little rental place at Algar Seco to round up the cats, and make sure we hadn't left anything behind. They all came when we called, and gradually, with a few stragglers, we got them into their travel boxes. As usual, Tink was the last to be caught but some well-placed tuna saved the day. We took a last look around.

"Bye-bye little house, thank you for not letting us down with dodgy plumbing or electrics."

A final look at the beautiful sea view and we locked up and left the keys in the post box as instructed. The cats were complaining loudly as we set off for the five-minute drive home. Home, we were going home.

We knew this would be a test as we didn't know how Barney would react to five cats, but as he didn't come into the house, and we planned to wait a week or two before letting the cats out, we had some time before we had to think about it too much. What we hadn't thought about was the lack of doors inside. The kitchen, bathrooms and bedroom were fine, but the living room had only saloon type doors, which left a gap at the top and bottom and didn't have any type of lock. We had to get used to closing the back door before opening the kitchen door and constantly herding cats back into the living room - and you know what they say about herding cats. Although we were heading into October it was still very warm and we were in danger of melting, keeping the house closed up all the time.

"I've had an idea," Nick announced, "if I cut some lengths of wood to about two thirds the width of the windows, we can slot them into the runners in the bottom of the frames, and open the windows enough to get a bit of a breeze, but not enough to let the cats out."

He showed me how the wood could stop the windows opening wider than we wanted, and made a note on his to-do list. This would be a temporary solution but we really needed a proper living room door. The opening was an arch, so the only solution was to have a door custom made. We asked around for recommendations and several people mentioned a carpenter who lived up in the hills beyond Silves. He was happy to take on the job and came down to take measurements. We impressed on him how urgently we needed it, and just over a week later he was back, complete with two doors, each glazed with eight small panels. After a little bit of adjustment, they were soon in place and a perfect fit. They looked great and the whole process had gone so smoothly. We weren't used to this.

Now the cats could be contained, we tried to bring Barney in at night. He wasn't used to coming inside and preferred to sleep on the front porch, wandering in and out of the garden as he felt like it. Our main aim was to keep him safe, and also to stop him from waking everyone up by barking out in the street at 3 am, but he wasn't keen. He was able to jump the low front wall, so off he went most days, just coming home for dinner.

Barney

He was still being fed by an elderly Portuguese couple who let themselves into the garden and emptied a carrier bag full of restaurant scraps into an old battered washing up bowl. This consisted of a mixture of chicken carcasses, rice, chips, and slices of bread and butter. Barney wolfed it all down, cooked bones and all, something we would never give our dogs, but he had obviously thrived on this diet for years. After a few weeks, we managed to make them understand that we would take responsibility for Barney now, and they no longer needed to feed him.

Barney's best friend was a Husky cross, called Nikas, who lived a few houses away. She was also an escape artist and regularly jumped walls and dug tunnels to run free with him. Her owner just couldn't find a way to keep her in the garden and eventually gave up, so she was another night-time barker. Now the cats were safely tucked up in the living room overnight, we tried to get them both inside, but it took a lot of persuasion and countless cubes of cheese and slices of ham to get them to even step over the threshold. The back door stood open all day when we were at home, and we took every opportunity to coax them in, but as soon as we tried to shut the door, Barney panicked and scratched madly to get back outside. This was going to take time.

The other issue was Barney's beautiful long coat, which was matted and full of grass seeds. He was quite a chunk and we didn't fancy trying to groom him ourselves, so found a mobile dog groomer advertised in one of the local papers and arranged an appointment. I explained that he was basically a street dog and not used to being shampooed and brushed, but Sergio agreed to come over and give it a go. He arrived a few days later and set up a table in the garden, laying out his shampoo, brushes and clippers while I filled a bucket with warm water. Barney was lifted onto the table, all 35 kg of him, I don't think anyone had ever lifted him before but whether it was the surprise at being hoisted onto a table or just his usual stoicism, he stood still and made no attempt to jump down. Sergio started to gently comb out his thick undercoat and realised that he was absolutely covered in ticks.

"Come and look at this!" he exclaimed, "I've never seen anything like it."

As he parted the fur I could see the swollen bodies of the ticks, with their heads buried deep in Barney's skin, it must have been so painful for him. Sergio brought out a bottle of surgical spirit and poured most of it into a large tumbler. With a specially designed tick removal tool, he started the slow process of easing the ticks out, taking care not to leave the heads inside. They are horrible creatures, parasites that drain their host of blood and we soon lost count of how many ended up squashed and drowned in the tumbler.

Two hours later, Sergio pronounced Barney a tick-free zone and lifted him down for a quick comfort break. It was tiring work and he hadn't even started to groom him yet.

Back up on the table, Barney was as patient as ever as his coat was shampooed, dried, cut and clipped. His calm acceptance of all this fuss and attention after years of street living was just incredible. There was no hint of aggression, not a growl or a whine, he must have sensed that it was going to be worth it in the end. At last, it was over and Sergio gave him a final spritz of doggy perfume before lifting him back down onto terra firma. Barney ran off, tail wagging, and promptly rolled in the dusty earth below the hibiscus hedge.

2

Windows

In the back of the wall that had been the reception desk, we found a phone socket, but when we plugged a phone into it, there was silence. I needed an internet connection, and we had a fax machine, so this was something else to be arranged as a priority. Portugal Telecom seemed to be the only option, so we went to their office to fill in an application form. There was no record of a line into our house, but there must have been one at some point in the past. They promised to send an engineer out to investigate.

He arrived a few days later and tested the line, as we had told them, it was dead. Off he went out into the street to find the start point for our connection. After lifting several man-hole covers in our road and out on the main road, he came back triumphant. As usual, it wasn't in the nearest, most obvious junction box, but further away, probably as our house had been built first, as the sales office, and had been the first to be connected. The wiring needed to be updated, but he had everything he needed in the van, so he set to work.

A few hours later we had a landline, an internet connection, and a wide variety of Portuguese TV channels. It all came as a package but as long as I could use my computer and fax machine, I was happy. He explained that we had free calls between 9 pm and 9 am, although I wasn't sure who I'd phone at that time of night, and produced our free cordless phone and telephone directory. I was used to a separate book for private numbers and a Yellow Pages for businesses, but this seemed to combine both. It was also quite thin and flimsy, I assumed it was just for the Lagoa area.

Later that evening I leafed through it, checking for any interesting information at the front, lists of emergency numbers, hospitals etc. As I read through, I realised, to my surprise, that it covered the whole of Algarve in one small book, maybe half the size of the one we had had in Berkshire. Mobile phones were just starting to become the essential piece of equipment that they are today and Portugal seemed to have 'jumped' the concept of landlines altogether. The country went more or less straight from public phone boxes to mobiles. Only the need for the internet fuelled the installation of telephone lines. Another thing I found slightly curious was the need to dial the area prefix, 282 in Lagoa, even if you were calling your neighbour across the street.

The postman came every weekday around 3 pm. When he had mail for us, he beeped the horn on his moped and shouted,

"Correio Senhora!" (Post!)

and I had to go out and collect the mail by hand. The first time it happened, I pointed out the brass 'Correio' plate on the letter box on the front door but he shook his head.

"Não, não posso." (No, no, I can't)

I didn't understand, he had to pass the front door to reach the post boxes, so it wasn't out of his way, but he wouldn't budge. He wouldn't push the letters through the letter box. He handed over our post, shrugged his shoulders, and drove the 10 metres to the row of official mail boxes. It's just as well I didn't press him on this point as, on closer inspection, there wasn't actually a slot cut into the door behind the 'Correio' plate, so he was right, after all, it wasn't possible.

A week or so later the post office in Lagoa had good news for us, they had post boxes in stock, and we could have one. Nick paid for it and was given a set of keys and told that it would be delivered and installed shortly. The next day a red van pulled up and ten minutes later we had our own post box. These small things seemed very significant at the time. Another sign that we were settling here and putting down roots.

Where to start with the house renovations? We had absolutely no storage, so we called on our carpenter to fit a kitchen and also install fitted wardrobes in the bedroom. This would allow us to unpack some boxes and make space in what would become the guest cloakroom/utility room. We also needed to upgrade the electrics, and worst of all, but definitely a top priority, cut two windows into the exterior kitchen wall. Which, of course, was curved. The house plans already showed the windows but no one had bothered to actually do anything about them. A lot of houses here are built with completely solid walls, and the doors and windows are cut in afterwards. I was dreading this. As much as I wanted natural light in the kitchen, and a view of the garden, I hated the thought of the noise, dust and disruption that it would bring. Nevertheless, we had to have it done, like a trip to the dentist, it loomed up as a necessary evil.

We were given the name of a local builder, Luís, who spoke pretty good English and would oversee the electrics and the window installation. He arrived bright and early one morning, bringing with him an older guy, maybe in his sixties, who spoke no English at all. We had a four-way conversation with Nick explaining to me in English, me telling Luís in semi-Portuguese, and Luís translating my Portuguese into proper Portuguese to his sidekick (we never did catch his name). Luís started measuring up on the inside and the outside of the wall, marking the proposed width and height of the windows in pencil. Nick kept repeating 'the curve, take the curve into account' as Luís nodded and drew on the wall.

"I'm not sure that's going to work," Nick said quietly.

"They must know what they're doing," I replied.

"Well, it would be fine if it was a straight wall."

"Yes, I know, Nick, it's a curve. We can all see it's a curve."

He went outside to look at the measurements once again.

Luís popped his head round the back door.

"I am going to confirm the window dimensions now, my colleague will start to make the cuts. See you later."

Nick came back inside looking troubled, as we heard the unmistakable sound of a heavy-duty grinder making contact with solid concrete. It screamed and whined and set my teeth on edge.

"I can't bear it. I'm going into the living room and turning the TV to maximum," I hissed and slammed the kitchen door, leaving Nick to it.

The cats were unsettled by the noise, some cowered behind the sofa, while others clung to me as closely as they could, hoping for protection. It went on for hours, and was so relentless that I realised that I had actually got used to it, and it had retreated to a background murmur. When the racket finally stopped it seemed strange and I almost missed it. I went out to the kitchen expecting to see two lovely empty holes, but the kitchen was in darkness as usual. Outside, I could see that some progress had been made, there was the outline of two windows, but none of the cuts had fully penetrated the wall. The machine had stopped to allow its operator to have his lunch.

Nick came back with his tape measure and worried expression.

"I still don't think this is going to be right," he whispered.

"But why?"

"Be.cause.of.the.curve," he hissed between gritted teeth.

"Ok, show me, explain to me so I can explain to him."

Nick looked around for inspiration. He picked up an offcut wood panel leftover from the kitchen installation and started sketching. He drew a semi-circle representing the wall, and a straight line representing the window.

"He's cutting it as if it was a straight wall, I know I keep saying it, but it's not going to work."

I looked at the sketch and it started to make sense, but how on earth was I going to find the words to explain what I still didn't 100% understand?

The noise started up again and I retreated to my safe space in the living room. Gradually I heard another noise punctuating the drone of the grinder.

Bang, bang, bang.

I looked out the living room window and saw Nick surrounded by more offcuts of wood, it looked as though he was making some sort of frame. Oh well, whatever makes him happy.

Another silence followed, I went out to inspect the progress.

The sunlight was blinding, there was a window-sized hole and I could see out of it, it was a miracle. I could also hear voices, one confident, one less so.

I dodged the rubble and took a closer look. Nick was holding his wooden frame up towards the gap, as the builder looked on, rubbing his forehead with a dusty hand. As one side of the frame sat flat against the opening, the other flailed in mid-air, proving that for the pretend window to touch each side it would need to sit at a ridiculous angle. Several times Nick placed the frame in the space and removed it, adjusting the angle each time and revealing the truth, that it wasn't going to work.

The builder and I had the same thought at the same time. I saw the light bulb moment cross his face as all became clear. Suddenly he was all smiles and nods.

"Pois, pois." (Yes, Ok) He grabbed the wooden frame and tried to slide it into place. "Não, não." (No, no.)

Nick mimed cutting away more of one side of the wall to accommodate the window. More 'Pois's' and work was back underway.

Nick smiled, "I think it will work now."

3

Work

I was still doing my three days a week, working with Edward at his estate agency, and Nick was able to book his work around the various tradesmen we employed, so life was very busy. On my days off, I concentrated on our rental apartment, answering enquiries and taking bookings. It was located on a development with a mix of holiday lets and permanent residents, right in the heart of the village, with a central reception where clients checked in and out and reported any maintenance problems. I knew the staff well as we had owned the apartment for five years, but now we were living nearby, I popped in more frequently. On one visit the office manager took me to one side.

"You know, I was thinking, your apartment is always full, don't turn any enquiries away, we have lots of apartments here, maybe we could work together?"

I hadn't considered building up the rental side, but actually, it could work well.

"That's a great idea, thanks."

We worked out a system for checking availability, and I started to plan an update to the information on my website. There was always a trickle of enquiries in September and October, usually repeat clients who liked to re-book straight away, to get their preferred dates for the following year. Then a bit of a lull until the post-Christmas rush. There was plenty of time to get photos of a few of the other available apartments, and some of the resort in general. There were swimming pools, tennis courts, gardens with towering palm trees and colourful hibiscus and bougainvillea, and a spectacular sea view from the frontline properties. It would give me a nice little project through the winter.

Once the carpenters and builders had finished the initial work on the house, we decided to start letting the cats out. Initially, we opened the windows for them to jump in and out, to avoid a bottle neck at the back door as Barney was now coming in more frequently and we wanted to give the cats an escape route, just in case. The first few days were a bit tense as Barney got used to them all running around, but after a couple of attempts to chase them, he quickly realised that he was outnumbered and gave up. As a newbie to cat ownership, the cats owning us of course, I still wasn't used to their freedom to roam, and lack of trainability. I was used to dogs, who stayed within sight, came when called (usually), and were basically much more predictable.

I tried cat-collars with bells attached, so I could at least hear them if I couldn't see them, but bought the quick-release type as I was paranoid about them getting caught on something. The quick-release feature was a bit too efficient and we found discarded collars everywhere. Neighbours would even hang them on the fence, knowing they had come from our cats. I then tried to train them into a kind of recall, calling 'ham' as I threw treats, hoping they would associate the word with the tempting nibbles. It worked, up to a certain point, but obviously only if they were nearby. I had to resign myself to letting them go and hoping for the best.

The first time one of them failed to turn up for dinner I was a mess. Of course, it had to be Camões, with his one eye. I called and called him, yelled 'ham' over and over, but by bedtime, there was still no sign of him. I woke several times in the night and crept out, hoping to find him curled up in the garden, but no. The next morning, I walked all around the local area, shaking a bag of cat biscuits, still nothing. Back home I couldn't settle to anything, I just wanted to know where he was and what had happened to him.

I heard my name being called and went out reluctantly, I was distracted and in no mood for idle conversation. Our next door neighbour was calling from the other side of the fence. We hadn't really met before as their house faced away from ours, with the front door on the opposite side. It was a large villa and Tom had told us that they ran it as a B&B.

"Hello, I am Gerhard, your neighbour."

"Hi, I'm Karen."

"I think you have some cats, yes?"

"Yes, we do." I hoped he wasn't going to complain about them digging in the garden, I really wasn't in the mood.

"Do you have a kind of black cat?"

"No, we have a black and white, a ginger, a tabby…"

"Not really black, but almost black, with small white stripes?"

Camões? Could he mean Camões?

"There is one which is a black and grey tabby, he's actually missing at the moment."

Gerhard smiled and clapped his hands, "Come please, we have a cat in one of the bedrooms."

I rushed out our gate and ran round to their front door.

Gerhard welcomed me in and explained.

"This bedroom, the first one on the right, the door was closed but the little window to the en-suite bathroom was open. We have clients arriving this afternoon so my wife went to check the room and found this."

He opened the door and out came the unmistakable aroma of trapped cat.

"Oh, I'm so sorry, is he still in here?"

"I think so, he ran under the bed when we came in."

I knelt down and peered into the corner and there was Camões, crouched against the wall. I was so relieved to see him, but also embarrassed to have to meet our new neighbours under these circumstances. I stood up,

"I think it might be best if we try to move the bed, I can't reach him from here and I don't think he'll just come to me."

With both the bedroom and front doors open, Gerhard nudged the bed away from the wall, and Camões took to his heels and ran out. I followed, hoping to encourage him back into our garden.

"I'm really so sorry, please let me know any cleaning costs," I shouted as I ran.

Naughty Camões, but at least he was back and safe, the dry-cleaning bill was a small price to pay. A few days later, I noticed a fine mesh had been installed across all the open ground floor windows.

Our other neighbours were a Portuguese family opposite, a Portuguese couple behind us, and a rental villa to the other side. There are pros and cons to living next to a rental. We found that they tend to be empty most of the winter, so you get used to the peace and quiet, then get a shock around Easter when the first holidaymakers arrive. There's generally a lot of noise on arrival day, which then settles down once the initial excitement wears off, and an occasional late-night a few days in, but even if they are extremely noisy you know they'll only be there for a week or two. We met Ana, who lived in the large villa behind us, several times and she was always chatty and pleasant. She had five or six dogs, which barked quite a bit, but as it was mostly during the day, it didn't bother us. Barking dogs are something you need to get used to in Portugal, it's just what they do.

It was a busy time at work and the serious buyers were out in force again. I showed an apartment to Anna and Simon, an English couple who were a similar age to us, and who were looking for a holiday home. We had quite a chat whilst they looked round, and discovered that they were also animal lovers with an assortment of cats, dogs and horses. After a second viewing they put in an offer, which was accepted, and we kept in touch throughout the buying process and celebrated with them when they finally signed the deeds.

4

Winter

The weather changed as November arrived, and we started to light the wood burner. Although not as attractive to look at as the one installed in the rental villa the previous winter, it was much more efficient, and the house was lovely and cosy. Barney finally gave in and spent the nights inside, lying in front of the fire as if he had always been used to this level of comfort, rather than sleeping on the front porch. He even allowed some of the cats to cuddle up to him, for extra warmth.

Little Minnie failed to appear for dinner one evening. After Camões's adventure, I didn't panic immediately, but when she wasn't around for breakfast the next morning, I started to worry. I printed out some posters and went around fixing them to lampposts in the area, and even put one in the window at work. That evening we walked miles calling for her, rattling a bag of cat biscuits and searching through long grass and under hedges. We traipsed across a building site nearby, in case she has got trapped or injured somehow, but there was no sign of her. Two days, then three passed. I was distraught, she was still young, about seven or eight months old and had recently been spayed. She was quite a homebody and she had never stayed away for so long. I was beginning to fear the worst. We spread the search wider, in case she had got into a car or van, and got lost. After a week, I received a phone call.

"Is it your cat that is missing?"

"Yes, it is, have you seen her?"

"I don't know if it is, or not, but there is a young black and white cat here, she appeared a few days ago and is very friendly."

"Where are you?' I was frightened to get my hopes up.

"In Sesmarias, at the reception for Presa da Moura, the new development of villas and apartments. She is living here in the office now."

Sesmarias was only a few miles away on the outskirts of Carvoeiro and on the way to Ferragudo. I picked up a cat box and went straight there. My heart was pounding all the way, hoping it was Minnie, but also scared it wouldn't be her. I parked outside the building and tried to compose myself before going in.

"Hi, I am the person looking for my cat," I explained.

"Ah yes, here she is," the receptionist lifted the cat up from behind the desk, and held her out to me. It wasn't Minnie. This kitten was mostly black with some small white patches, Minnie was the opposite.

"Oh, I'm sorry but that's not my cat." I was so disappointed, I had known it was a long shot, but had been hoping so desperately to see her.

"I'm sorry too, but I had to call you to check."

"Yes, of course, I understand, it would have been awful if she was here and I didn't know."

I took the kitten and gave her a cuddle, she immediately started purring and buried her face in the crook of my elbow. I scratched behind her ears and she turned her head, pressing it into my hand. She wasn't Minnie but she was still a little one in need of a home.

"Do you want to come with me?" I asked her before looking up at the receptionist, "Can I take her?"

"Yes, of course, we don't have the conditions for her to stay here, if you want to take her, I think that would be good for her."

I popped her in the box and drove home, with tears rolling down my face. She was a gorgeous kitten, who we named Cindy, very affectionate and cuddly, but sadly we never found Minnie or discovered what had happened to her.

As we prepared for our second Algarve Christmas, we took a trip to the relatively new Algarve Shopping mall in Guia. The Continente supermarket there was huge, much bigger than our local Intermarché, and with the other shops, food court, and cinema, you could easily spend a whole day there. It was one of the first malls in the Algarve, and quite a curiosity. We bought a few Christmas presents, then went to see what festive delicacies we could find. As we approached the fresh fish and meat counter there was an overpowering smell. An area had been cleared and a tall Christmas tree erected, but it wasn't a green tree, it was almost white. The smell was stronger now and on closer inspection, we realised that the 'tree' had been constructed from bacalhau, dried salt cod, a staple food in Portugal, and the traditional choice for a Christmas feast. It was quite surreal, as we watched, several people approached the display and removed a triangular-shaped fish, then bashed it against the nearest hard surface. Those that passed the test would be taken to the counter to be weighed and priced. Those rejected would be returned to the display and another piece chosen for the strength test.

It is said there are enough different bacalhau recipes for every day of the year, and it appears on virtually every Portuguese restaurant menu, but it can be an acquired taste. We decided to stick to turkey for our Christmas dinner. We were also surprised at how quiet it was, having been used to queuing just to get into the car park at our local M&S and Tesco, from mid-November onwards.

One year we had gone shopping very early on 23 December, about 5 am, and it was still packed. A staff member came out from the stockroom carrying several large trays of brussels sprouts, but by the time she got to the display, there were only a handful of nets left to put out, the rest had been grabbed as she made her way through the store. Here it was just an ordinary day, with no queues, plenty of parking spaces, and straight through the checkout.

Edward had decided to go away for a couple of weeks over Christmas and New Year, and although the estate agency office was officially closed for the majority of his absence, I was left in charge. I popped in to check emails and post every other day, as we had several sales going through, and we didn't want any hitches or delays. Early on the 28th of December, we were woken by a tremendous thunderstorm. The rain was torrential and we could hear it drumming on the windows, accompanied by constant flashes of lightning and deep rumbles of thunder. The garden was filling up with water, rushing like a river around both sides of the house. It was impossible to step outside, such was the force of the deluge. I had honestly never seen rain like it.

We didn't get much sleep and even in daylight, the storm continued at full strength. By mid-morning, the rain started to ease up a little and we went out to check for damage. The house was ok but the roads were covered in fallen branches and streaks of sand and silt. The drains were full and water was spewing out of the manholes in the road, in an endless cycle of flooding. My phone rang,

"Hello, it's reception here, the apartments in your block are under water, can you come and help?"

"Yes, ok, we'll try to come down, but I don't know if the roads are clear."

We took it very slowly, water was still rushing to the lowest point on the in and out roads, and there was a real danger of aquaplaning down the hill. The storm had combined with an unusually high tide and as the sea reached the top of the beach, it met the floodwater and forced it back along the streets. As we entered the apartment building, we found a waterfall gushing down the internal staircase. The electrics were out so there were no lifts, and our apartment was on the third floor. We had to fight against the water as we climbed flight after flight of stairs, and by the time we got to the apartment we were soaked up to our knees.

There was a bustle of activity in the building. All the front doors had been flung open and the maids had been despatched with mops, buckets, floor mats and towels, to try to soak up as much of the water as possible before it did any more damage. Our three bedrooms on the fourth floor were inches deep. Although the balconies had drainage holes, they weren't big enough to cope with this amount of rain, and the water level had risen to the point where it had found a slight gap in the patio doors and then poured in, across the bedrooms, down the stairs and out into the corridor and the main staircase.

We rolled up our jeans and started mopping, allowing some

of the maids to move on to other apartments. It was hard work and extremely slippery, so I found it much easier to work barefoot. It took several hours to get the situation under control when suddenly something occurred to me.

"Nick, I think we had better check the Estate Agents."

Although the door was at street level, there were two or three steps down into the shop, and the door wasn't a great fit. I hadn't given it a thought before, in the chaos, but I dreaded to think what we would find there.

I checked my handbag; thank goodness the keys were still there from locking up the previous day. I rushed out and flew down the road, every shop, bar and cafe I passed had flooded. The rain had now stopped and the sun was out, so the pavements were full of tables and chairs, cushions and rugs, anything that could be picked up and moved was laid out to dry. I reached the estate agent's and could see straight away that the carpet had come loose and was floating in several inches of water. I had to start again. I was already exhausted from clearing the apartment, my arms and legs ached as if I had been wading through thick mud.

I stepped down into the icy pool. A mop was no use, it was just too deep to have any effect, and being below street level meant the water was contained, with no way to let it escape. The only option was to empty bucket-fulls down the toilet and hope that the drains had begun to clear. Nick arrived about half an hour later. Anne-Marie and Steve had turned up to help and had taken over in the apartment, so he had brought another bucket, and started emptying it out through an open window and into the street. By mid-afternoon we had to stop, we just didn't have the strength to carry on.

Fortunately, all the paperwork on top of our desks had stayed dry, but there were two filing cabinet drawers to be tackled and the carpet was still sodden and curling up at the edges, but we would deal with all of that tomorrow. We left the aircon set to 'dehumidifier' and went home. The next morning we were back, armed with Stanley knives to hack great chunks out of the carpet, revealing a tiled floor below. The office was starting to smell of wet dog as we hauled the dripping lumps up the stairs and onto the pavement. The council had arranged for collections of all the damaged property, so the streets resembled a junkyard of abandoned belongings.

The tiles were much more attractive than the burgundy carpet and I hoped Edward would decide to keep them rather than replace the carpet. The filing cabinet drawers were crammed with ancient property details, thankfully nothing of any importance, and were so wet that they had moulded together with their cardboard folders to make oddly shaped papier-mâché models. We filled several bin bags with them.

It was extremely hard work, especially after the previous day's efforts, and I was glad to lock up and forget about it for a few days.

This type of flood was actually quite a regular event, there is a tile on the wall opposite the chemist that records the water level during one such event in November 1987. The water reached about waist height and once again many of the shops, bars and restaurants were inundated. The out road used to be an inlet channel, similar to the one in Ferragudo, which allowed for a high tide. However, once cars became more common transport than donkeys, it was turned into a road, hence the tendency to flood.

Nick had always been fascinated by a 'For Sale' sign on an anonymous door a little further up the out road. It had been there for as long as we could remember, with a faded sign saying 'Discoteca'. The door was secured by a chain and padlock, and we had never seen anyone go in or out. When he was still deciding what kind of job or business he wanted to do, he rang the number out of sheer curiosity. The person who answered said he was in Lisbon, but would travel down the following weekend, and could meet us on Saturday afternoon. He arrived on time in a very smart car and impeccably dressed. He spoke perfect English and explained that he was an art and antiques' dealer, and had many international clients.

"Please excuse the mess, but this place hasn't been used for many years," he unlocked the padlock and chain, but struggled with the door. "As you can see."

After a few minutes, the lock yielded and the door creaked open. Inside there was a staircase leading down to what had been the underground disco, an ideal location to avoid annoying the neighbours. It was like stepping back in time, with faded velvet tiered seating leading down to a central dance floor, and a DJ booth to one side, still equipped with turntables and records. It was as if the last customers had just got up and walked out and left everything where it lay.

He explained that it lay below the mains drainage system, so a pump had been installed to deal with any flooding incidents. However, during one flood there was also a power cut so the water just kept pouring in and it hadn't been used since.

Nick was stunned, it was completely different to what he had imagined, and there were possibilities, but renovating it would be a huge investment, let alone the issues of planning and licences which can be a nightmare. Reluctantly, he decided that it was just too much of a gamble, but often when we walk past, even now, he wonders whether he should have pursued it further.

5

New year

We hadn't made any plans for New Year's Eve, but Nick bumped into Kurt and Monica from Cheers while we were cleaning up, and they told him about their plans for a buffet at the bar. It sounded perfect, casual and relaxing, just a few drinks and an informal meal, so we booked for us and mum and dad. The next day we could hardly move, every muscle ached, so we rested up ready for our night out.

On arrival at Cheers, we were met by Kurt handing out glasses of champagne and directing us to the buffet table. They had prepared large bowls of chilli and rice, a whole poached salmon, various salads, cheeses and cold meats, and pride of place, Kurt's favourite, an English Gala Pie. Most of the other guests were German and there was much excitement at the prospect of the 'entertainment'. There had been no mention of entertainment when Nick had spoken to them, and it's not a very big place, with no space for live music or any kind of performance. It was all a bit confusing.

As it got closer to 11 pm, midnight in Germany, the large TV on the wall was switched on and everyone gathered to watch. Maybe it was going to be a firework display or a concert. With a cheer and a round of applause the programme started. It was in black and white, and in English, but none of us had ever seen it before. Monica couldn't believe we didn't know it.

"But it is English, and old, I think it is from the 1960s."

We shook our heads,

"No, I've never seen it or heard of it."

"It is a German tradition, every year it is on TV and so popular, everyone watches it."

"But why?"

She shrugged, "I don't really know, I thought you would?"

I couldn't help but laugh at the thought of millions of German households waiting for this old black and white show every New Year's Eve.

We watched as the story unfolded. It was called 'Dinner for One' starring Freddie Frinton as a butler and May Warden as the lady of the house, Miss Sophie. She is celebrating her 90th birthday and the table is set for 5, however, her guests have already predeceased her, and the butler has to impersonate each one as each of four courses is served, along with four different drinks, champagne, wine, sherry and port. He becomes increasingly drunk and continually trips over a rug, and starts to mix his words up. The catchphrase was shouted out along with the TV:

"Same procedure as last year Miss Sophie."

"Same procedure as every year."

The whole bar was in hysterics as the programme finished, with the pair of them heading upstairs towards the bedroom. Living here does give an insight into other cultures, not just Portuguese.

At the beginning of 2005, Edward returned from holiday, and I decided to call him to break the news of the flood before he came into the office.

"Oh, my dear, I had heard there was a bad storm, but I didn't realise it was that bad. I only arrived home a couple of hours ago, and oh the jet lag, I'm exhausted."

"Yes, I'm sure. It was pretty exhausting clearing up the office too."

"Of course, I can't imagine, however did you cope?"

"Well Nick helped a lot, but there are still things to sort out, be prepared when you come in tomorrow."

The next morning, he arrived, and scanned the office, taking in the exposed tile floor and the damp smell which still lingered.

"Oh, thank you for doing all this," he waved one arm around vaguely, while the other hand covered his mouth in shock.

"I took some photos for the insurance claim," I said, passing an envelope over. "You can see how bad it was."

He shuffled through the photos, gasping and sighing at each one.

"How terrible, what a shock it must have been."

"Yes, it was a bit," and I went on to explain about the apartment and the indoor waterfall.

He grabbed a chair and slumped down with his head in his hands.

"And there I was on holiday, enjoying myself and I had no idea what was happening here. I'm so sorry."

"You weren't to know, it's one of those things."

"But I feel so bad, let me know how much time you both spent here and I'll make it up to you."

"It's ok," I replied, not terribly convincingly, it would be nice to feel that our efforts had been appreciated.

"You know, I think those tiles look really attractive, much better than the carpet, don't you think?"

"Erm, I don't know, let's give it a few days to get used to it, we'll have to wait for the insurance claim before we do anything anyway."

After a few days, Edward made a decision.

"Do you know, I think you're right, the floor is better like this, it's lighter and brighter, I think we should just get a nice rug instead."

Before we knew it, it was Carnaval again, and we took advantage of a day off to sit at a cafe on the out road and watch the procession. We got home about 5 and I was just about to start feeding the cats when we heard a screech of brakes and a loud cry. Rushing out into the street we saw a car stopped at the corner, and Barney running off onto the open land opposite. The driver shouted that Barney had just appeared in front of him and he'd had no time to stop, it was just a glancing blow, but we could see drops of blood on the road. In a panic, we ran across the road, following the same direction, and soon found him lying in some dense undergrowth. He was shaking, in shock, and blood was dripping from his mouth, he was also holding one of his front legs at an odd angle. We got him back up onto his feet and helped him home. We started to check him over and were relieved to see that the blood was coming from a small cut on his tongue, and there were no signs of internal bleeding, but we had to get his leg examined and make sure he hadn't suffered any other injuries.

I rang the vet, not expecting a reply on Carnaval, but maybe there would be a message with an emergency contact number.

"Estou." (Hello?)

Thank goodness, Dr Carlos was there. I explained what had happened and he said we could bring him straight up. I sat with Barney in the back seat, trying to reassure him, while Nick drove as quickly as he could. Dr Carlos was waiting at the gate and between them, they carried Barney inside and onto the examination table. After feeling the paw and leg, he diagnosed a dislocated shoulder and took an x-ray to confirm it. We were so relieved that there was nothing broken, but I couldn't stay and watch while the joint was manipulated back into place. Nick is not as squeamish as I am, and stayed to help keep Barney calm.

They soon emerged, Barney looking much happier, with a bandaged leg and shoulder, and Nick a few euros lighter. I decided we weren't going to go through this again, from now on Barney would be kept in the garden, his wandering days were over. The gate was closed at all times, and we installed a fence on top of the front wall. There would be no more jumping in and out as he felt like it, but it meant Nikas couldn't get in and out either, or so we thought.

Nikas had other ideas. She was not going to be split up from Barney, not for a single day. The first evening that the new regime was in place we were in the living room when we heard the metallic clang of the gate, then a heavy thud. On investigation, we found Nikas running around the garden, playing with Barney as usual. When she had had enough and felt like a wander, she jumped onto the narrow edge of the gate, teetered for a few seconds, then jumped down onto the pavement. The gate was about four feet high, and only a couple of inches thick, but she never missed. No wonder her owner had found it impossible to keep her in.

With more properties available for rental, and the busiest time of year approaching, I decided to hand in my notice to Edward. Not only did I have access to the majority of the apartments on the development, via reception, but I had also been approached by several individual owners, including Anna and Simon, and had built up a portfolio of rental properties. I had promised myself to give it at least a year at the estate agency, and incredibly, that time was up now. Edward was very disappointed and tried to persuade me to stay on, but I had made my mind up. I had been used to working for myself from home when we had our metal finishing business, and when I taught English as a Foreign Language, and although I enjoyed the job, I found it difficult being constrained by set working hours. I really wanted to concentrate on building my rental business, and reluctantly, Edward accepted my decision, and advertised for a replacement.

Julie was the successful applicant, and we overlapped for a week. It was strange being the trainer rather than the trainee and I realised how much information I had absorbed in the last 12 months. After my final day at work, I handed my keys back with a feeling of relief, but also a little sadness; it had been an enjoyable time on the whole. Edward took Nick and me out for dinner to a restaurant in Porches, to show his appreciation. We had a lovely meal and parted as friends. I still popped in to say hello when I was passing, and always got a great welcome. I had become one of the people that I had noticed when I first started work. Edward would break off from what he was doing, beckon me over to his desk, and ask,

"So how are you, and Nick, and how is business?" Then tell

me about the properties he had taken on, and the sales he had made.

It was nice to see Elaine and Julie too, plus Anne-Marie was still there a couple of days a week, so I remained very much part of the family.

We saw an advert for a charity fundraiser being held in a bar in the village, in aid of the local Bombeiros. We were keen to go and support it as my dad had been in the Fire Service, and we knew that the Bombeiros relied on donations to afford vital equipment. There was a quiz and a raffle, and one of the organisers, Steve, came round selling tickets at each table. We started chatting and found out that he had taken early retirement from the Fire Brigade in Soho, London, and had recently moved to Carvoeiro. He lived just down the road from us and we swapped numbers, so he could let us know of any future events. The bar was quite small, but there was a good turnout, and the Bombeiros gained several hundred euros.

We also started to get to know more of our Portuguese neighbours further along the road. To our surprise, we recognised quite a few of them who had businesses in the village, and our dog walks started to take a little longer as we stopped to chat. It was good for my Portuguese as they all treated me as an equal, and didn't slow down or change their vocabulary for me. I had to learn to keep up, especially when there were a few of us in a conversation.

Another year, another lost cat. This time it was little Cindy who went out one morning and didn't come back. It was heartbreaking to lose another one.

But it didn't stop me from trying to save more kittens. A message caught my eye whilst scrolling through the Carvoeiro chat room, a photo of a beautiful fluffy kitten, and a post looking for a good home for him. He looked so cute I couldn't resist giving them a call.

"My husband was driving home yesterday afternoon when suddenly all the traffic stopped. He got out and went to see what had happened, and this kitten was sitting in the middle of the road. He picked him up and brought him home, and we will keep him if necessary, but we already have ten cats."

Ten cats, I thought, madness.

We arranged to go and see him that afternoon as they were only about a five-minute drive from us. The door was opened by a tall, slim, blonde woman, we guessed she was Dutch from her accent.

"Please come in, here he is, isn't he adorable?"

We followed her into the living room to find the kitten balancing on the back of the sofa. He was truly adorable and I picked him up straight away.

"He's gorgeous, we have four cats that we have rescued, but I can't resist him, can we take him?"

"Of course, I will be very happy to know he has a good home."

"We will take good care of him," I assured them.

Nick just raised his eyebrows; he knew that coming to see him meant that we would be taking him home.

"We have named him Fluffy but of course, he doesn't know it yet."

I looked at the kitten with his relatively huge paws and tail, and the name Harry sprang to mind, from the film 'Harry and the Hendersons' about a Bigfoot/Yeti type animal who was adopted by a family. Our new arrival was a real character who made himself completely at home with us. He made friends with all the cats, and Barney, and was always up to some sort of mischief, pouncing on our feet or climbing up our legs, whether we had trousers on or not. As he grew, his coat got longer and fluffier, and he was a big boy, very similar to a Maine Coon. We didn't drop the 'Fluffy' name completely, although we thought Harry was more dignified for such a magnificent cat, it did evolve into Harry ze Flooff, as a nod to his Dutch rescuers.

Harry

Nick's mum, Elsie, decided she wanted to spend more time in Carvoeiro after spending a week with us in our first rental villa. As she was planning to stay for at least eight weeks, she wanted to rent her own apartment in the centre of the village, so she could walk to the local shops and cafes and have her independence. Anna and Simon's place was ideal. It had two bedrooms, two bathrooms, a fully-equipped kitchen, UK TV channels and a sunny balcony. There was also a lift in the building, and it was only a few minutes' walk from the beach.

Her first trip was in the spring of 2005, and as soon as she returned home, she asked me to book her in again for that autumn. This became a regular pattern over the next few years eventually including a month over Christmas and New Year too. She just loved the pavement cafe lifestyle, which she had got used to when Nick's dad worked abroad for many years, first in Italy and then in Germany. Sadly, he had died just a few years into retirement, but she had many happy memories of the time they spent abroad.

Her routine was to walk along to Smilers cafe every morning at 10, having stopped to buy a newspaper or magazine on the way. She always sat at the same table and spent the morning reading or doing a crossword, only stopping for a spot of people watching as she drank her coffee. If she was still there approaching lunchtime, she would treat herself to a gin and tonic, or glass of wine, before making her way back to the apartment to spend the afternoon sitting out on the balcony. We took her out to restaurants a couple of times a week, and quite often on a Sunday, we would invite her and my parents to our place for a BBQ, but she was just as happy pottering about on her own, as long as she had a good book to read.

My 40th birthday was approaching and it was almost two

years since our move to Portugal. Time for a party, as we had celebrated all our milestone birthdays since we had been together. For Nick's 30th we had taken over a small country pub for the evening and hired a new-fangled entertainment called Karaoke. We filled the pub with family and friends and took turns at the mike, wondering if it would ever catch on. For my 30th four years later we hired a skittles alley attached to another country pub and had a fun evening, with prizes for the winners.

Nick's 40th came around quickly and we literally pushed the boat out for this one with a cruise down the Thames from Windsor to Maidenhead and back. There was a buffet and disco upstairs and a bar and seating area downstairs. As his birthday is in the middle of June the weather was beautiful and we had a great vantage point to admire all the beautiful houses that border the river. Some of the residents obviously enjoyed seeing the pleasure cruisers on summer evenings and waved and raised their glasses to us as we passed by, while they sat in their gardens with a sundowner cocktail or preparing a barbecue.

My birthday is in early October, the beginning of autumn in the UK but in the Algarve, it was still late summer. We had often spent this time of year here anyway, staying in a rented villa for a couple of weeks holiday. Even our very first trip had been on my birthday, and we left the U.K. for good on the day after my birthday. Following in the tradition of taking over a local pub for the night we asked Kurt and Monica in Cheers if they could host the party. They were more than happy to oblige and organised a delicious buffet for our guests. The celebrations continued for nearly a week with friends and family from Portugal plus those who made a special trip to be with us.

6

2006, Lisbon

The beginning of the year brought a very unusual visitor to the Algarve, snow. Although it regularly snows in the Northern part of Portugal, and you can ski in the Serra de Estrela, we rarely even see a frost. However, a grand total of 2 cm fell on the higher ground around Monchique, and schools closed to allow the children to take a day trip to experience the snow. For most of them, it would be the first time, as it was over 10 years since the Algarve's last snowfall.

Back to house renovations and we decided to tackle the second bathroom. The first step was to empty it, so we bought a self-assembly shed for the garden and moved our boxes into it. All the pipe work was still there, and there was even a mirror on the wall, but we had to reinstate the sanitary ware and get it plumbed in. While we were in a state of upheaval we might as well re-tile too and get rid of the dated beige and pink colour scheme. We called in Luís again, and he provided a plumber and a tiler. We planned to move the washing machine in here and put a dishwasher in the kitchen, so it would become more of a utility room.

With so much work going on, and the water being cut off for hours at a time, we decided to go up to Lisbon for a few days. Barney and the cats went into Jan's kennels and cattery in Vale d'el Rei and we set off on the Alfa pendular train from Tunes. It's an excellent service, very reasonable and easily the best way to get to Lisbon, and on to Porto.

We had rented an apartment close to the Rossio, or Praça de D. Pedro IV, to give it its full title, and took a taxi from the rank outside Entrecampos station. It dropped us off a few hundred metres from our destination, a narrow, cobbled lane that was impossible to drive down. The owner of the apartment met us, and showed us up the uneven staircase, to the first floor. Although it was located in a very old building, the apartment itself had been tastefully modernised and was clean and well-equipped, and included a welcome pack of essentials.

The open plan living room/kitchen featured a huge window with a magnificent view of the square below, the ruins of the Castelo de São Jorge to the left, and the ruins of the Convento de Carmo just visible to the right. It was an excellent base for exploring the city.

Donna, an American, offered to show us around, so we left our luggage and followed her downstairs and back out to the lane. We reached a stone staircase, set into the hill and started our descent. At the bottom was another lane, and another set of steps, and then a third set, which brought us out into the corner of the Rossio. Looking back and up, she pointed out our living room window, it seemed impossibly high and I wasn't looking forward to the return trip, up all those stairs. The first thing we saw was a narrow shop directly opposite, with quite a queue of people waiting outside.

"That looks popular," I remarked.

"Yes, there's always a line there, they serve shots of the Ginginha cherry liqueur from the window, for 1€ a glass."

I made a mental note to stop there on our way back for fortification before our steep climb home. We turned into the square, which is similar to Trafalgar Square in London with large fountains and a statue of D. Pedro himself. Donna pointed out the D. Maria II National Theatre to our right, and at the opposite end, the arch which gives access to Rua dos Sapateiros.

"That's a long, straight, pedestrian-only road with tables and chairs down the middle belonging to the cafes and restaurants that line both sides of the street. There's a great choice of places to eat there."

Now we had got our bearings, Donna left us saying, "Don't forget, if you need anything, just give me a call."

We strolled around the edges of the square, admiring the imposing architecture, then turned off into the warren of side streets. Tiny shops squashed together selling everything from expensive jewellery and bridal gowns, to specialists in umbrellas, gloves of all colours, and one with an amazing display of shower caps. We carried on down Rua de Prata to the Praça do Comércio, which is a huge square overlooking the Tagus River, bordered by very grand buildings which previously housed government offices. It was busy with plenty of people jumping on and off tour buses.

We picked up a timetable and booked tickets for the following day. Suddenly tired from our journey and early start, we turned back towards the Rossio and hauled ourselves back up to the apartment for a rest. The steps were a killer, we would have legs of steel by the time we left.

Rested and refreshed we went back down to explore further and find somewhere to eat. This time we turned right, behind the Theatre and into another maze of tiny streets. We passed an Italian restaurant that looked interesting and smelt even better, as a garlicky, herby aroma wafted around the tables outside. Nick asked a waiter about availability, but they were fully booked, so he went inside and made a reservation for the following evening. We ended up in a small, traditional Portuguese place nearby, serving pork with clams, cataplana and seafood rice, all the well-known and well-loved local dishes. It was a warm June evening and we sat outside enjoying the food and the lively atmosphere.

The next morning, we had a quick breakfast of coffee and pastries on Rua dos Sapateiros, on our way to pick up our tour bus. It was another bright sunny morning, ideal for sightseeing. From the Praça do Comércio we drove along the riverfront towards Belém. It was further out than I thought, looking at the map, but as we passed the 25th April Bridge, we could see we were getting close. We got off to investigate the Descobrimentos monument, celebrating the explorers who set off from Portugal to discover new lands, then crossed over to the Mosteiro dos Jerónimos. The monastery contains the tombs of Vasco de Gama and our friend, Luís de Camões, the one-eyed poet and namesake of our one-eyed cat.

Back on the bus, we travelled to the north of the city whilst listening to a recording recounting Lisbon's history, and pointing out places of interest. It was getting hotter now, so we got off at the next stop and sat down at the first cafe we came to, grateful for some shade and a long cool drink. Nick's phone rang, it was Luís.

"Hi, is everything ok?"

"Yes, everything is fine here. How is Lisbon?"

"It's great thanks, we're really enjoying it."

"Very good. I have one small problem, well not really a problem, but, the floor, is completely concrete."

Nick was confused, of course, the floor was concrete. I could see he was concerned but he stood up and walked a little way away from the noise of the traffic, and the background buzz of the cafe. By the hunch of his shoulders, it didn't look like good news. After a few minutes, he finished the call and came back to the table.

"Luís says the soil pipe from the old toilet has been filled with concrete, he's not even sure which direction it goes. It looks like they'll have to take the whole floor up to try and figure it out."

"Oh.'"

"He'll call me later once they've had a better look. Thank goodness we're up here and not trying to live through all that."

We spent the afternoon slowly making our way back to the apartment. Still taking in our surroundings and enjoying our time, but also wondering just how much time and money this would add to the job. We had only planned to stay here for two more nights and didn't relish the prospect of returning to a full-scale building site. That evening we ate at the Italian restaurant, and couldn't help discussing the possible outcomes.

"I suppose if they really can't sort it out, we'll have to abandon plans for a second loo," said Nick glumly.

"I hope not, that's been one of the things I've been looking forward to, a guest loo and utility room. We'll have to find some way round it."

"It depends how long it's going to take, and how much it'll cost. We can't just keep digging forever."

"I really don't want to give up on it though."

I had had such high hopes when we moved in, and less than 18 months later we had come up against our first real obstacle.

The next morning, we hiked all the way up to the Castelo de São Jorge. It sits high above the Baixa area of Lisbon and was a much tougher climb than we expected, but the views from the top were magnificent. We could see across the river to the Cristo Rei statue on the opposite bank, down into the Rossio, and across to the rooftops of the Chiado district. I remembered doing a Portuguese language course back in the 90s, with cassette tapes and a textbook. One of the sentences I learned, that stuck in my mind was:

"Onde fica o Castelo de São Jorge?" (Where is St Jorge's Castle?)

I practised it over and over, following the pronunciation on the recording, and was quite pleased with my achievement, only to find out that it was in Lisbon and not the Algarve, so I would have no opportunity to deliver the question to locals on our next holiday, amazing them with my knowledge of the language. I had had to settle for 'Onde fica o supermercado?' instead, but now I finally knew where the Castle was.

We walked back down through the Alfama district, the oldest part of Lisbon, and famous for Fado music. It was extremely quaint and picturesque but we were still preoccupied with the situation at home.

"I'm going to have to ring Luís again soon if we don't hear from him first," said Nick.

"Yes, you had better chase him up. I would have thought there would be some news by now."

"I'll give him until this afternoon, he'll be at lunch now,"

Nick replied, looking at his watch.

By 3.30, he couldn't wait any longer and dialled Luís's number.

"Hi Nick," he answered. "How's Lisbon?"

"Fine, just like it was yesterday, more to the point, how is our bathroom floor?"

"The floor? It's good, we find the old pipe and dig out the cement, so we make a new connection now."

"So, it's fixed?" Nick was incredulous, and I watched his expression anxiously, for confirmation.

"Yes, all ok now, we plan to tile tomorrow then when it is all dry and set, we can install the toilet."

"That's great news, but I thought you were going to call and tell me."

"Sorry but we have been working hard and as everything was ok I didn't want to, erm, destroy, no, disrupt your holiday."

"Well thank you, but I would have preferred to know what was happening."

"Don't worry, enjoy Lisbon, see you tomorrow."

We celebrated that evening with a meal at a Fado restaurant and toasted our new bathroom/utility room with a glass of port.

7

Bombeiros

Nick was still working for the local sofa and bed shop and met so many people on his deliveries that he was becoming quite well known. He would often be asked to remove the old pieces of furniture that were being replaced, some went to the dump in Lagoa, but those that were still in good enough condition, he offered to local charities, or sold to raise funds for charity. His phone rang one day, it was Steve from the Bombeiros fundraiser.

"Hi mate, I just wondered, we're trying to get hold of some furniture, armchairs or sofas, maybe a table, to make the Fire Station rest room a bit more comfortable, have you got anything suitable?"

"Er, maybe, I'll have a look and see what's in the store room. What sort of size?"

"Do you want to come and have a look at the room, see what might fit in?"

"Yeah, I'll pop round later, 3 o'clock ok?"

"Great, see you later."

Nick pulled up and saw Steve waiting for him outside the vehicle bay.

"Alright mate? Thanks for doing this."

"No problem, let's have a look and see what I can do."

Steve led Nick through the station and into the room where the bombeiros waited in between calls. It was quite sparsely furnished.

"I was just thinking it would be good to get some more comfortable seating, we can be in here for a while, of course, it depends on how busy we are, but…"

Nick looked around; it wasn't a bad size.

"There is a sofa I took away a few days ago, it's still perfectly usable but the people who had it have just had new curtains made, and they decided to get a new sofa to match. Do you want to see it, it's just in storage near the shop?"

"Yeah, great, I'm sure the lads won't care what it looks like."

Nick took a few measurements then they both jumped in the van and went to check it out.

"Yes, I think that will fit ok if we move the dining table along a bit," said Nick, wielding his trusty tape measure.

"Brilliant, if I give you hand, can we take it over now?"

"Yeah, it will only take half an hour or so, we might as well while we're here."

So, they loaded up and went back to the station. A few of the guys helped to re-arrange the room, and the sofa was installed in pride of place. One of the 'guys' was actually a girl, Steve introduced her as Maria, a bombeira who spoke excellent English and was helping him with his Portuguese. She was really grateful to see the sofa in place,

"That looks great, thank you so much, we will all really enjoy it," she said.

"I can't believe we got it sorted so quickly," replied Steve, then he slapped Nick on the back,

"Cheers, mate."

Nick had done his good deed for the day.

The new curtains he had mentioned were made by Lynne, who had moved over from Scotland just a year or two before us. She was a talented seamstress and offered a made to measure service. Nick had met her in the sofa shop when she was in the middle of an order for a large villa on one of the local golf courses. The clients wanted new curtains and curtain poles for every window, plus Roman blinds in the kitchen and bathrooms.

"I don't know how I'm going to manage," she said wearily, "the curtains are almost ready, but I can't do it all on my own, I'll need someone to help with putting the poles up, and carrying the curtains upstairs, they weigh a ton. I don't suppose you'd be able to help, Nick?"

"Well, I don't mind a bit of DIY, is the place empty? Could we go and have a look, see what it involves?"

"Aye, I've got the keys, they said just to help myself. They're not due back for a couple of months. Would you really be able to help?"

"I'll give it a go."

And so began Nick's career as a curtain pole installer. Who knew he had so many talents?

I first met Lynne when one of my apartment owners asked me to organise a quote for new curtains. We met at the apartment and I waited as she took the measurements, then we discussed the owner's requirements. She was very easy to talk to and it felt as if I had known her for years. A few weeks later mum decided she would like some new curtains and matching cushions, and so we introduced her to Lynne, and she became a family friend.

Many of the people Nick met went on to become friends, one such couple was David and Marianne. They were very hospitable and enjoyed entertaining, as Marianne was an enthusiastic and talented cook. I first met them at a birthday party they were hosting for a family friend, who was staying with them for a holiday. There were about twenty of us, including the birthday girl and her husband and children, and another friend, Pam, who was a regular visitor. It was a lovely warm evening, and after a delicious barbecue, birthday cake and plenty of local beer and wine, one or two of the guests decided to take a moonlight swim. Those who were staying at the villa went and changed into their swimming costumes, while the rest of us sat around chatting.

"Are you not going in, Karen?" asked Pam as she re-appeared, ready for a dip.

"No, I haven't got a swimsuit with me, don't worry, you go in, I'm happy to stay here."

"Come on, it will be fun, I've got a spare costume you can borrow, we look about the same size."

"No, I'm fine here, honestly."

But she wasn't taking no for an answer and I found myself changing in her en-suite bathroom. When I emerged, I could see lots of heads bobbing about, and two men standing at the edge of the pool ready to dive in. I looked around for Nick, but the rest of the place was deserted. One of the men dived in, the other jumped, and I saw a flash of familiar boxer shorts. The men who weren't guests at the house had all decided to strip off to their underwear, I was just glad that was as far as they went.

Nick's transport business was going from strength to strength. Sometimes he needed an extra pair of hands and called on Anne-Marie's partner Steve to help out. Then came a job that needed even more manpower,

"I wonder if I should call the other Steve, the bombeiro, what do you think?"

"There's no harm in asking, I suppose it depends on his shifts?"

"I'll give him a call, if he doesn't want to do it maybe he'll know someone else."

Steve did want to do it, so Nick had a choice of Steves, both happy to do a few hours with him, now and again.

The summer of 2006 was dominated by the World Cup. Football is a huge thing in Portugal, it is almost a national obsession. Every cafe and bar has a TV to show regular matches, and for big occasions, restaurants install them too. We have even seen small crowds gathered to watch re-runs of old matches after the season has ended. As we have residents from the UK, Ireland, Germany, France, Brazil, Spain, The Netherlands, Russia, Ukraine, amongst many others, the rivalry was fierce and all the bars advertised the upcoming matches, while drivers fixed their home nation flags to their cars. When Portugal was playing, and especially when they won, you could hear the car horns all over the village, late into the night. Even in defeat, however, I have never seen any violence or bad behaviour, just some good-humoured banter between the different nationalities.

Nick and Steve had become quite friendly, after working together a few times, and although I'm not a football fan, we arranged to go out for a drink and to watch one of the England games.

"Is it ok if I bring someone with me?" he asked.

"Yes of course, who is it?"

"Erm, you remember Maria? The bombeira at the station?"

"Oh yes, just good friends?"

"Yeah, something like that."

I was pleased that I would have someone to talk to, as I knew they would be more interested in watching the football than chatting to me.

We got to the bar in plenty of time to make sure we got a table. I didn't want to be too close to the action, so chose one at the edge of the terrace, where Maria and I might have a chance of hearing each other. We saw them park the car and start walking towards us. Maria was very petite, with shoulder-length dark, curly hair, and a wide, friendly smile.

"So nice to meet you both."

She stretched up on tip-toe to kiss Nick on both cheeks, then greeted me in the same way, and sat down next to me. She didn't look like a firefighter, she seemed too delicate for that type of work. We ordered some drinks and Nick and Steve started discussing England's chances, but I was keen to find out more about Maria.

"So, you're a bombeira? I would never have guessed. How

did you get started, have you been there long?"

"Well, it's a bit of a long story."

"That's ok, we've got a couple of hours at least."

"That's true," she laughed.

"So, my son was in an accident a few years ago, and I had done a first aid course and was able to keep him going until the ambulance came. You know the ambulance comes from the fire station."

I shook my head, "No I didn't know that."

"Yes, the bombeiros do lots of things apart from actual fires."

"Oh, really, I had no idea."

"So, they came along with a doctor on board, and by a miracle, he survived. It was an English woman, a nurse called Val, who started the first aid classes, and she held them at the station. After the experience with my son, I decided to try to help more people, so I asked the Chief if I could join as a volunteer."

"Wow, that's amazing."

"I love it, I went on to do an advanced first aid course and then started to go out with the crews. In the beginning, I was doing one day a week."

"Gosh, I don't think I could do that, you must have to go to some difficult situations?"

"It can be, but someone has to help these poor people who have been in an accident or taken ill," she shrugged. "My very first call was to a hit and run, and a man was lying in the road.

He looked very bad, there was lots of blood. I looked after him until a doctor arrived, and we put him on a stretcher and off to hospital. I was nearly sick but I thought, if I can do this, I can make a difference, and I did it," she smiled at the memory then put her hand on my arm. "And two weeks later, this man, he phoned from his home in the Alentejo, to thank us for helping him."

"So, he was ok?"

"Yes, he was, and so thankful, I'll always remember that day."

I was astonished, she was so brave, but told the story so humbly.

"So, are all the bombeiros volunteers?"

"Some are, but a lot are paid now. I am full time and paid now, since last year. I had to train for fires too, but I'm not so keen on that. I prefer the ambulance work, but I do it when it's needed, like in fire season."

I hadn't heard of fire season.

"When's fire season, in summer?"

"Yes, usually around May to September or October, it can depend on the weather and how soon the temperature drops and the rain starts."

This was fascinating, I was learning so much. It was half time and the boys finally remembered we were there.

"Ready for another drink?"

"Yes please, all this talking is thirsty work," Maria laughed. "Hey Steve, remember when you first started, oh it was so funny."

Steve rolled his eyes, "Oh that was terrible."

"What was?" I was curious now.

"You know caracóis? Snails? Well, the chief had some and offered one to Steve," she was really giggling now and Steve was shaking his head. "You know Steve doesn't like that kind of thing, but he didn't want to look bad in front of the rest of the crew, so he ate it, then was almost sick straight away."

"Ah, but I got my own back, didn't I?"

Maria giggled again.

"We normally go to the Fatacil restaurant for lunch, and I started making chip butties with the bread rolls. They were all looking at me the way I looked at the caracóis. Anyway, the next shift, one guy decided to try it, then another, and eventually I got them all making chip butties."

I couldn't imagine a bunch of Portuguese firefighters tucking into chip butties, the idea was hilarious. The second half started and we went back to our conversation.

"So, you met Steve at the station?" I asked.

"Yes, as I spoke English well, they paired us up. Then I started to give him Portuguese lessons and taught English to the Portuguese, so if they arrived at a call from a foreign person, they could talk to them better. Even German or Dutch people can usually speak English better than Portuguese."

"So, tell me, are you just colleagues?"

"Well," she glanced across at Steve, who was engrossed in the match and quite oblivious, "we have become quite close. In fact, we are talking about moving in together."

"Oh, that's great, congratulations!"

She smiled shyly, "We haven't really told anyone yet, but we will soon, then we'll have to work separately, which is a shame, but I understand the reasons."

They seemed comfortable with each other, and happy together. They were both divorced and with children from their previous marriages, so I was pleased and hoped things would work out for them.

On one of my regular trips up to the vet, I saw a poster looking for a home for two kittens. They had been found in someone's garden and handed in. One was white and tabby and the other black and white. We were up to five cats at this point, but what was two more? I brought them home and named them Smokey Joe and Polly. They were about three months old and very closely bonded. They settled in well with the other cats, and Barney was getting used to new arrivals and barely seemed to notice that his family was growing.

The next of our cats to disappear was Ginger, Camoes's brother. He was always very adventurous and had gone missing for 24 hours at a time, but the days went on, and he didn't come back. More posters, more searching and waiting, another sad mystery.

8

Nick, all in a day's work

As well as the normal transport jobs and house removals, Nick has often had some more unusual requests. Josie was probably in her 80s, an interesting and well-travelled woman who had settled in the Algarve. For a change, she decided to spend a few months of the winter in the south of France, so Nick transported some of her possessions across for her, while she and her little dog, Fleur, travelled by plane. Just a few weeks later he received a phone call.

"Hello Nick, it's Josie here. I'm afraid it's just too cold here, I thought it would be more like the Algarve, but it's really not. I think I'd like to come home."

"Ok, that's a shame, but I can come and get your things, when are you flying back?"

"I think I'd rather go by road this time; it will be less stressful for Fleur."

"I don't think the van will be very comfortable for you, it's a long way, it will take two or three days."

Josie thought for a moment. "What about hiring one of those people carrier things, I'll just bring back the essentials?"

"I'll look into it, but it will probably work out quite expensive."

"Don't worry about that, I'll cover any expenses, and I do like a road trip."

Nick got a few quotes for a rental that would let him take a vehicle through Spain and France, and Josie was more than happy to go ahead, so off he went to pick them up. They had a great trip back, Josie was fascinating company and entertained him with tales of her days as a travel rep in the 1950s, leading tours around Iraq, Syria, Jordan.

"You know, all the places you hear about in the news now, they were beautiful countries, lovely people, wonderful food."

She had sent us a bank transfer to cover the cost of the trip, plus fuel, hotels etc, and had wildly overestimated what would be needed, so we popped over one Sunday morning to return the surplus. We pulled up outside her apartment, the front door was open and Fleur came running out, making a beeline for Nick. He picked her up and carried her back inside, while she yelped with joy, and covered his face in kisses. Josie was sitting in a high-backed chair by the open patio doors.

"Ah how lovely to see you again," she smiled. Then to me, "Come over here my dear, where I can see you better."

I moved closer and she looked me up and down, sizing me up. We had been married for around 20 years at that point, but it felt as if I was meeting the parents for the first time, waiting for her approval. Nick had sat down on the sofa opposite Josie, and Fleur was still jumping up and down, and twirling round in front of him.

"We do love Nick, don't we Fleur?" Josie giggled. It seemed I was the gooseberry here.

I must have passed the test though, as we had a lovely afternoon, chatting about their trip and hearing some more anecdotes about her life. After tea and cakes, she leaned towards me and winked as she said,

"My dear, do you know, you chose very well."

Steve and Maria moved in together and as they were just down the road, we saw them fairly frequently. Maria was now driving ambulances and small fire trucks, the first woman *bombeira* to do so in Lagoa. It was hard to picture as she was so petite. As well as attending emergencies, she was also responsible for transporting patients to hospital for appointments or blood tests and sometimes did two or three return trips to Lisbon in a day. They invited us over for a barbecue and I asked how her week had been.

"Oh, it's been non-stop, I've been up to Lisbon so many times, I could drive there in my sleep. We had a new-born baby who was so sick he had to go to see a specialist paediatric cardiologist and it took us seven hours to get there because his condition was so delicate, and there were so many machines monitoring him. We brought him back the same day, another seven hours, but it looks like he'll be ok, so that's good. Then I was called out at 4 am, to an elderly woman in Lagoa. It was so dark and her house was in a country lane, but we were told to turn at the blue gate. We drove up and down looking for a blue gate, but couldn't find it, then we saw a woman walking across a field towards us. I got out and asked if she was waiting for an ambulance, and she was. I asked about the blue gate and she looked confused, "oh that gate fell down years ago." I had to stop myself from laughing."

"Was she ok?"

"Yes, I checked her over and didn't find anything, but she complained about her leg so we went to the hospital. As soon as we went in, they recognised her and even knew her name. I think she was just a bit lonely and maybe has some type of dementia. It's very sad but we never know, so when we get a call, we go."

Steve had also been busy, with all his training and experience in London, he had started organising drills and training sessions and got hold of some donated gym equipment.

"And we have got a fridge and a microwave in the restroom too, and I put some curtains up," added Maria. "It's looking a lot nicer now, and we can make something to eat when the cafe is closed."

I admired their dedication to the job; it was more of a vocation.

We decided to take our first holiday since our move to Portugal. The quietest time of the year for rental enquiries and bookings is mid-November to mid-December, so that meant it would have to be a long haul to get some good weather.

We settled on LA, with a cruise down to Mexico, then some relaxation at the Beverly Hilton Hotel and then at Shutters on the Beach in Santa Monica. Barney and the cats were looked after by Jan again, and mum and dad came round to check on Nikas and feed her. She was still jumping the front gate but there's no way she would have put up with being confined to kennels. We had a great time and the two weeks flew by.

We returned home late in the evening and planned to pick them all up the next morning, but as we unlocked the door, a brown tabby appeared and brushed against my legs. We put some food out for her and she devoured it hungrily. She wasn't exactly tame, but neither did she run away, she seemed to have moved in while the house was empty and quiet. We brought the other cats, and Barney back the next day and surprisingly, they all ignored her. We named her Missy, and she took to sleeping on the top of the wall behind the shed, so we put a cat box there, with a blanket and a waterproof cover, and it became her domain. She kept to herself, not causing trouble but not going out of her way to make friends either, she seemed quite happy to just mooch about.

At the beginning of December, we had another almighty storm, thankfully this time our apartment was unscathed, but the centre of the village was flooded once again. The sea had covered the beach, carving out large ruts in the sand, and then invaded the square, leaving sandy deposits behind when it finally retreated. I was grateful to just be a spectator this time, and not responsible for any of the clean-up operations.

Elsie arrived in the middle of December, for a month's stay. We took her to one of the beach restaurants in Galé for lunch on Christmas Eve. The weather was spectacular, the sun was almost blinding in the deep blue sky, and the sea glittered. As we sat on the terrace peeling fresh prawns, washed down with a dry white wine, she looked around at the sunbathers below and announced,

"I don't think I would be doing this back at home in Crowthorne."

Just over a year after we lost Minnie, we found Polly dead on the road. Again, it had happened just after we started letting them out, and only a couple of months since she was spayed. It's so difficult to lose any of them, but I found it easier to accept when we knew what had happened and weren't constantly looking and waiting for her, wondering if she was trapped or in pain somewhere. As so often happened, we soon found another kitten in need of our help.

9

2007, Kitten love

Nick left for his annual golf trip at the beginning of May as usual. For ten days I would have sole charge of the cats and dogs, plus dealing with all my rental clients. It was a busy time as the final payments became due, and I was still receiving last-minute requests and bookings. In the evening, I took Barney and Nikas out for a walk onto a nearby patch of open land. It was still warm and sunny and they enjoyed running free, sniffing all the different animal smells and following the scent trails of rabbits. It was quiet, well away from any roads or houses, and as I stood and watched them, I heard a faint noise. It sounded like a baby crying, I looked around but there was no one to be seen. I heard it again and moved towards the sound, a regular, insistent little squawk every few seconds. It seemed to be coming from a patch of thick undergrowth. I pulled some of the branches apart and saw a tiny kitten, all alone, right in the middle.

There was no way I could carry her home, especially with the two dogs beside me, so I called them and hurried back to the house to pick up a travel box. Leaving the dogs secure in the garden, I retraced my steps, hoping the kitten was still there. As I got nearer, I could still hear her crying, I put the box down, knelt on the rough grass and searched for her. She was sitting where I had left her, waiting for me to come to her rescue. She didn't move as I edged closer, just stared up at me with big blue eyes. I had thought she was pure black but could now see touches of brown and cream, a little tortoiseshell kitten. I reached down and picked her up with one hand, she didn't struggle at all as I popped her into the travel box, but she did keep up a steady cry all the way home. My phone beeped with a text from Nick,

"Landed. All fine. All ok with you?"

"Yes fine. You'll never guess…"

We called her Coco and she lived a rather eccentric life, spending most of her time on top of the kitchen cabinets.

A few weeks later we noticed Barney had a lump on his rear end, just under his tail, so off we went to see Dr Carlos again. He diagnosed a hernia, which would need surgery and booked him in for the following week. I felt so guilty when it came to dropping him off, not being able to explain why there had been no breakfast for him that morning, the poor boy looked very confused. When we picked him up that evening, he was still drowsy, but managed a tiny wag of his tail, partly due to the anaesthetic and partly to the bandage which was wound round his back and between his legs, to hold the dressing in place.

Dr Carlos explained that it was quite a deep wound and it was important to keep it covered as best we could. It was in such an awkward place, he had to be able to walk, pee and poo, but also protect the stitches until the wound had healed. A further indignity was the lampshade collar, which limited his vision and kept getting stuck in doorways. He must have wondered what he had done to deserve this treatment.

We went back and forward every other day for the wound to be checked and re-dressed, but it was very slow to heal. It seemed that every time he sat or lay down, the stitches opened up again. Then we noticed that the bandage was cutting into the top of his leg, so it had to be abandoned. We tried to think of an alternative and eventually came up with a solution; a pair of Nick's boxers. We manoeuvred Barney's back legs into the pants, cut a hole for his tail and unbuttoned the fly, and there he was. His wound was protected without being tightly bound and the boxers were loose enough to let the air circulate. It also meant that we could take his lampshade off, as he could no longer nibble at the dressing.

I had been at home with him for weeks now; we couldn't leave him as he still panicked if he was alone in the house, and in the garden, there were too many opportunities to cause further damage to his stitches, but I was going stir crazy. We decided to take him down to the village and sit on the terrace outside "A Vela" restaurant, to give us all a bit of a break. He walked around proudly in his Calvin Klein's and was quite the talking point as Antonia, the other diners, and even passers-by noticed his outfit, and Barney enjoyed all the attention. From a street dog to designer togs.

My parents had now moved out to a typical Portuguese house in the countryside, about a 20-minute drive from Carvoeiro. Their Portuguese neighbours were very friendly and welcoming. They had quite a lot of land and grew lots of different fruit and vegetables, mum and dad would often find a bag of lemons, or a cabbage and some 'favas', broad beans, hanging from their gate. There was also a constant supply of fresh eggs, and a jar or two of home bottled olives. There were some language difficulties, as the neighbours, Maria and Reinaldo, spoke very little English, but mum took the opportunity to improve her conversational Portuguese and they managed to understand each other pretty well.

Maria called across excitedly one day, clutching a cardboard box. Mum went over expecting some eggs or dried figs, so was surprised to see two kittens inside.

"They come from my friend's farm, one boy, one girl, brothers."

"They're lovely, how old are they?"

"'I think six weeks, very pretty?"

"Yes, they're beautiful. Are you keeping them?"

"Yes, they stay here with us, Beca and Charlie. My friend's child named them."

The kittens grew quickly and were always around the gardens. They began to pop into mum and dad's place, oblivious to their two dogs. After about six months mum asked if they were going to be neutered. Reinaldo laughed,

"No necessary, brothers."

"Well brother and sister," mum replied.

He nodded, "Brother and sister, no necessary," and wandered off.

A little while later, it became apparent that it was necessary, but also too late, as Beca grew a very fat, round tummy. As she lay on their sofa, mum could see tiny movements below the skin,

"I knew it, brothers, indeed."

Beca grew and grew until she could barely waddle around. She spent most of her time in mum and dad's spare room, rearranging blankets in preparation for her babies' arrival.

I got a text message early one Saturday morning. 'Beca's

started having her kittens, two so far.' Quickly followed by, 'Three now.' Half an hour later,

'I think that must be all of them, she's quiet now and the babies are feeding, she's a great mum.'

We were all relieved that mum and the babies were doing well. Three hours later, 'Number four has just appeared. And five. Six, she's had six.'

Five were either pure black or black and white, and one was a brown tabby, we're not quite sure where he came from. Charlie seemed to know they were his kittens and lay curled around them protectively, as they lined up at the milk bar. Maria and Reinaldo were astonished at the news, but happy for mum to look after the little family, and to re-home the kittens when they were old enough. Beca was a great mum and the kittens grew quickly. Their ears and eyes opened, and as they started to move around, their little personalities began to show. At about 8 weeks they were weaned and ready to find new homes.

We made posters and put them up in the vet clinic, and spread the word far and wide. One person took the two black and white ones, a boy and girl pair, and a family wanted the little tabby boy. Mum planned on keeping two, but the enquiries dried up, so she shrugged and kept three. Jet, Tina (Turner), and Elvis, who looked like he was wearing a white jumpsuit, but had black patches across the top, and down both sides of his head. Beca and Charlie were quite happy with their little family and showed no signs of going back to their original home. They took the kittens over to show them off but always came back to mum and dad's. How to go from no cats to five, in one easy lesson.

One of my apartment owners phoned in a panic.

"Karen, please can you help?"

"If I can, what's the matter?"

"I was just coming back to the apartment when I saw a car slow down beside me, and a little kitten jumped or was thrown out."

"Oh no, is it ok?"

"Yes, I caught it and carried it home, but it is so small, and I can't risk it being here."

The apartment was open plan, and on the 4th floor, I could imagine it would be difficult to keep a small kitten inside.

"I go back to Germany next week, as you know, what shall I do?"

I could guess what was coming next.

"Do you think you could take it for me, and maybe find a home?"

"Well, I'll try, but you know how difficult it is."

"I know, but please?"

"Nick, can you get the cat carrier out?"

He went and picked her up, she was a tiny tortoiseshell who we named Bella. Of course, no one came forward to take her, so once again, she stayed. When I took her to the clinic for her vaccinations, Dr Carlos was accompanied by two student vets. He introduced them as Filipa, his daughter, and her friend, Renata. They had been studying in Brazil and were due to qualify in the next few months, but had come to Portugal for some work experience. The girls seemed so young, but I guess it was just me getting older. I hoped Filipa would come to work with her father, but she told me their next placement was in Seville where they would be working with horses, which were her favourite animals.

One of my very first clients in our apartment, Steve and his wife Linda, had become regular visitors, coming back every year with various combinations of friends and family members. This year, they had a more unusual request for me. Their eldest son was getting married, and the couple wanted to spend their honeymoon in Carvoeiro. So far so good.

"Could you organise accommodation for around 24 people?"

"For a honeymoon?"

"Yes, they want to bring close family and friends with them too."

"Ok, let me see what I can do."

Our apartment was free, as was Anna and Simon's, so that was ten people accommodated. I checked with reception, we would need another 3 bed, plus 2 more 2 bed apartments for the rest of the group. With a bit of juggling, we managed it and left it to Steve and Linda to allocate guests to apartments. As well as the accommodation, I helped with transport to and from the airport, restaurant bookings, and tee times for rounds of golf. The wedding would take place on a Saturday in July, then they would fly over the next day, ready to carry on the party.

Everything went to plan, and they arrived on Sunday afternoon. Their first meal was at Tia Ilda, overlooking the beach, and I had arranged for the dining area on the roof terrace to be decorated with flowers and swathes of white fabric, which were tied around a wooden pergola. Everyone was in good spirits, and after a delicious meal came the final surprise, a three-tier cake, finished with whipped cream and fresh fruit, and local fizz to toast the happy couple. We joined them again later in the week for drinks and karaoke, then waved them off at the end of their stay. They had all had a wonderful time, and enjoyed a memorable holiday, and it was one of my more unusual bookings.

Elsie had spent her usual two months in Carvoeiro and was preparing for the journey home. She made a final visit to Smilers, said her goodbyes to the staff and other regular customers, and enjoyed a gin and tonic on the house, for her last drink. Nick picked her up in the afternoon and drove to Faro for an evening flight back to Gatwick. As they approached the airport, a heavy sea mist rolled in, but the check-in desk was open and operating as usual. He said goodbye and she went off towards security in her airport-provided wheelchair assistance.

I was at home, keeping an eye on the flight departures board online when it suddenly flicked from 'wait in lounge' to 'cancelled'. I refreshed the page. Now more flights were showing their status as cancelled too. Another refresh and the airport was closed. The fog was too dense, and it was already 9 pm, there would be no departures tonight.

I tried Elsie's mobile, but she must have already switched it off in preparation for boarding. I tried calling the airport and the airline, but they were continually engaged. I had no idea if they were planning to take the passengers to hotels or just leave them in the airport overnight, but Elsie had some mobility problems and neither would be suitable for her. Nick was nearly home, so I waited for him to arrive while trying to think of solutions. Her apartment wasn't an option as new clients had already arrived, and I didn't have anywhere else she could stay. I started to phone local hotels and B&Bs but there was either no reply or they were full.

I heard the car pull up outside and went out to tell Nick the news.

"But I've just left her, everything seemed fine."

"Well, it's not. I've tried to get more information but I can't get through, you might have to just turn around and go back."

While we were discussing the options his phone rang. The screen flashed 'Mum'.

"Yes, yes… Ok… yes. Karen saw it on the website. No, no, I know, ok." He finished the call, and opened the driver's door, 'I'm going back, she's told them she can't go into a hotel unless it has disabled access rooms and they've said they'll get her suitcase and meet me at the departures check-in area."

"But where will she go, we don't have room."

"I know, keep trying hotels, anywhere between here and the airport."

Back on my phone, I went through the list I'd made earlier. No reply, no vacancies, no reply. Finally, a response,

"Hello, do you have a disabled access room available for tonight? Yes, tonight, I think it might be close to midnight before they arrive."

Hooray. The Mirachoro on Estrada do Farol had a room available. I texted Nick and told him just to get back as soon as possible.

The next morning, Elsie decided that she wouldn't have breakfast in the hotel, but would still go to Smilers for coffee as usual. She sat at her usual table, ordered her normal galão, and waited for the reaction. All the staff were amazed.

"But, you left, we said goodbye."

"Yes, but the fog had other plans. I'm going back tonight instead."

That merited another gin and tonic on the house.

As she didn't have an apartment to relax in, my parents entertained her for the day, with lunch at Algar Seco Parque, and then it was time to set off for Faro again. This time all went smoothly, and she arrived home none the worse for her extra day in the sun.

10

2008, Puppy love

My dad was diagnosed with Parkinson's disease in his late 50s, which had been fairly well controlled by medication, but since moving to Portugal he had been referred by our local hospital to a specialist unit in the Hospital de São João in Porto. It was a teaching hospital attached to the university, and the Professor of neurosurgery had a particular interest in Parkinson's and was involved in pioneering research. They offered my dad the chance to participate in the programme and he started on the tests, scans and examinations which would decide whether he was a suitable candidate for surgery.

Porto is about six to eight hours from the Algarve, either by train or by car, and it means travelling virtually the full length of Portugal. There followed many trips, usually just involving an overnight stay, until he was told that, yes, they felt he could benefit from the surgery, and did he want to go ahead. He didn't hesitate, even though it was still fairly new and experimental, he wanted to be part of the programme. He was added to the waiting list and advised that it would probably take place in about six months.

"Oh, I'm so pleased to see you today," said the pharmacist.

"Thank you, it's nice to see you too," smiled mum.

"No, I really am pleased, I want to talk to you."

"Ok, what's wrong?' Mum assumed it was something to do with the prescription she had come to pick up.

"I know you have dogs and I need help."

"Dogs, right, so it's not about the tablets?"

"No, it's my son."

"Your son? Not a dog?" The conversation was getting stranger.

"It's my son and a dog. Sorry, you know we had that storm in the night? Well, my son was walking home from a bar, in the rain, when he saw a tiny puppy sitting in a puddle by the side of the road."

"Oh, really? How small is it?"

"Tiny, really very tiny." The pharmacist picked up the small sheet of paper that was the prescription and placed it on the counter. "She could sit on this, just this paper. Tiny. He picked it up and put it inside his jacket and brought it home to our apartment, but we didn't have any dog food so we gave it some chouriço."

Mum smiled inwardly at the idea of feeding chouriço to a puppy, but they had tried their best.

"But we can't keep it, I work here full time and he studies and goes out with friends, and we are in an apartment. Do you think you can help me find a good home?"

"Well, I'll try. We already have a new puppy, we have only had her for two weeks, and we have our older dog too."

"Oh, thank you so much, I don't know what else to do. Can you come back this afternoon? I could go and get her at lunchtime?"

Mum agreed and went back a few hours later, expecting to see a normal puppy, assuming the pharmacist had exaggerated how small the pup was, to make her seem more cute and tempting. However, when she walked back into the pharmacy, the woman picked up the smallest puppy she had ever seen, wrapped in a football scarf.

"Here she is," she announced proudly, and handed over a little black and white baby, barely bigger than a guinea pig, and with a suspiciously orange stained mouth.

"Oh, she really is tiny, isn't she?" The puppy gave mum a little garlicky kiss, and her future was secured.

An hour later I got an email with a photo of my dad holding the pup, his hands looked huge beside her tiny frame.

"Guess what?" read the message.

"Who's that?" I replied.

"A lost puppy, we've taken her in."

"Oh, can we come over and see her?"

As soon as Nick came home, we drove over. We knew Barney was an older boy, and Nikas wasn't really ours, so I was quietly hopeful that we could take her, but I had to have a chat with mum and dad and see if they would rather keep her. She really was the cutest little thing, if a little nervous, but then she'd had quite a rollercoaster ride for the last couple of days. There had been no sign of her mum or any siblings and we had no idea how she had come to be found on her own in a puddle. She must have been terrified.

"She's gorgeous, isn't she?" Mum handed her to me.

"Oh yes, I just love her, what do you think Nick?"

"Yes, she's lovely," he smiled, knowing what was coming next.

"How is she with Molly and Daisy?"

"They're all fine together, she's been sleeping cuddled into Molly."

"Oh, that's good."

Or was it? Was I being selfish taking her away from a home where she would be loved and cared for? And with a little playmate too?

"Are you planning on keeping her?" I asked.

"Well, we will of course unless you know of anywhere better she could be?"

I looked at Nick, then back at Mum.

"Well, we would be happy to take her, if you think that would be ok for her? Or would she be better here with Molly?"

Mum smiled, 'If you want her then take her, we'll be able to see her and maybe one pup is enough for us to look after and toilet train and everything, and we don't want Daisy to feel pushed out."

So that was it decided, Maisie, as we named her, was coming home with us. Barney welcomed her happily, always the gentleman and the cats were all bigger than her, so that was fine too. She was hilarious, such a little time-waster, skipping around and rolling on the floor with her toys. A few days later I took her up to Dr Carlos for the usual check-up and to see if she was old enough to start her vaccinations. She easily fit in a cat box, so I brought one into the living room and set it down on the sofa, while I picked her up, found her favourite blanket and popped them both in the box. It seemed a bit heavier than I expected, but maybe she was just starting to grow and put on weight now she had a regular supply of dog food, instead of chouriço.

Inside the clinic, I placed the box on the examining table and gently lifted her out. Dr Carlos examined and weighed her, pronounced her healthy, but advised that we should wait another week or so before starting her injections. As he went to make out a card for her, his assistant, a small, gentle soul, tapped my arm.

"E o gato?" (And the cat?) She asked.

"Não gato, cão, cachorro," (Not cat, dog, puppy) I smiled. I knew she was small but it was obvious she was a puppy and not a cat.

"Pois, mas o gato?" (Yes, but the cat?) She asked again, pointing to the cat box.

"Sim, gato," (Yes, cat) I laughed, yes it was funny to bring a dog in a cat box.

"Mas o gato. Vacina?" (But the cat, vaccination?)

"Não, vacina na próxima semana." (No, vaccination next week)

She looked disappointed. I wasn't entirely sure why.

I paid for the consultation and opened the cat box to put Maisie back inside, and suddenly everything became clear. Sitting right at the back of the box was Coco. She must have snuck in while I was getting Maisie and the blanket, no wonder

I thought the box was heavy. I turned to Dona Isabel, who was now laughing at the shock on my face.

"Gato," I said apologetically "não sabia." (I didn't know)

She found this hilarious and regaled Dr Carlos with an explanation. He looked at her, then me, and gave an uncharacteristic grin. I now had no choice but to put them back in together for the journey home. I slunk out in my embarrassment, howls of laughter following behind, but the girls travelled together quite happily.

Nikas and Maisie

Around this time, my back problems were causing me significant pain, and I spent a lot of time resting on the sofa. Maisie was excellent company, and so small that I could still pick her up easily, and she loved to climb up onto the sofa beside me. One afternoon, Nick arrived home from work, and as he walked into the living room carrying a cool box, he announced,

"I've brought you a surprise."

"Oh lovely, is it a Magnum ice cream?"

He shook his head, opened the box, and out popped Skip. Skip was a gorgeous silver tabby that Nick had found sheltering under a large communal bin in Albufeira marina. He was just about to throw some packaging materials away when he heard a little cry. He couldn't see anything inside the bin, so started to investigate further, and found this tiny kitten, all alone. The kitten allowed himself to be caught easily but Nick had no cat box with him. It was a blistering August day, and all he had in the van was a small cool box that had contained his lunch and a water bottle. He had been working with fireman Steve, and his son Billy, so they held him while Nick drove home. As with so many of our rescues, we advertised online and put posters up in the clinic, but no one wanted little Skip, so he stayed. When I went to hand in the posters I was met by the new Dra Filipa, she was joining her father at the clinic after all.

Steve called round one day, looking a bit down.

"Are you ok?" asked Nick.

"Yeah, well no, I don't know. I think we'll be going back to London soon."

"Oh."

"Yeah, mainly for the kids and their education, it will just be for a few years, I hope, but I think it's the best thing for them."

It was a hard decision, but they had to put their family first. Maria's children were half British and wanted to live and study there, and although Billy had been at a Portuguese school and spoke the language fluently, it would be good for him too. It was still sad to see them go, and we promised to stay in touch.

As I began preparing for my spinal fusion surgery, my dad was also preparing for his brain surgery. It was a scary prospect as the operation would be carried out while he was awake. The surgeon would need to ask him to perform certain actions during the operation, to check he was working in the correct part of the brain. Dad was undeterred.

"Even if it doesn't help me much, they might find out something that means someone else can get better treatment in the future."

Attached to the hospital were a small shopping centre and an Ibis hotel. Mum booked a room for the first week, and dad was admitted as an in-patient for the first time.

The surgery was performed successfully, and Paulo, one of the nurses, stayed with him throughout, chatting away about football. Dad would have to stay in hospital for a while, so he could be monitored and assessed, but once he was feeling a bit better and able to get up and walk around, mum was offered to share his room, on a pull-out bed. She left the hotel and joined the hospital world as a strange hybrid of not being a patient, but not just a visitor either. It wasn't something they offered very often, normally just to parents of very sick children, but they made an exception for patients who had travelled a long way.

In the next room, there was a Portuguese couple in a similar situation. José and Maria were from the Azores and had stayed in the hospital before when José had undergone the same brain surgery as dad. They were now back for a few days, for a check-up. Maria was an old hand at the hospital system and soon shared her knowledge with mum.

"You know we can use the staff canteen? And laundry, what are you doing about clean clothes?"

"I'm taking them to the dry cleaner in the shopping centre," mum replied.

Maria let out a gasp, "That's so expensive, I will show you the best place."

The next day mum gathered up a bag of washing and they left the hospital by the back entrance. Along the street and round a corner, chatting all the way, they came to a self-service launderette.

"This is the best place, I come here all the time."

There was a bank of coin-operated washing machines on one side, and tumble driers facing them on the opposite side. Maria went to get change from a machine on the back wall, and two doses of washing powder and fabric softener while mum started loading the machines. When she had finished, she looked up and saw that Maria was still wrestling with the change machine.

"What's wrong?" she called.

"This machine has stolen my money."' She was banging it on the side and rattling the drawer.

"'How much did you put in?"

"The machines take 50c coins so I put in a euro, but only one 50c came out."

"Here take this," mum held out another couple of euro coins.

"No, it has taken my 50c, I don't want it to take your euros and do the same thing."

"Has it ever done it before?"

"No."

"So maybe it was just once, let me try."

"No, not until I get my 50c, we could lose all the euros!" Maria could not be persuaded to try again. She looked around and saw a number written above the change machine. "Ah there is a number, for emergencies, I will call them." She fumbled in her bag for her phone.

"I think an emergency is if the machine is broken and you can't open it, or if it floods the shop…"

"This is also an emergency, they have stolen 50c!"

"But I've got more, it's not a lot to lose, 50c doesn't buy much now."

"In that cafe across the street, I can buy a coffee and a cake for 50c, or two hot waters with lemon."

"Let me try one of my coins, and if it happens again, we'll phone the number."

"Ok, but if they steal another 50c…" Maria shook her fist at the machine.

Two euro coins produced four 50 cents.

"It seems to be working now, I'll go and start the washing," said mum. Maria followed, muttering under her breath.

Now that dad was making a good recovery from the surgery, the doctors encouraged him to take a short walk every day, just around the hospital corridors. He wasn't allowed out yet, but it was important to see whether his walking was improving, and to maintain his muscle strength.

In the out-patients' department, there were some vending machines with the usual snacks and soft drinks, and mum and dad made it part of their evening stroll. There were security guards stationed at the doors which separated out-patients from the wards, but as they were both in pyjamas and dressing gowns, they were allowed through. After a few of these trips, the guards started to recognise them, and wish them 'Boa noite.' The next evening one of them asked which ward dad was on.

"Neurology," he replied, pointing to the scars on his head.

"Oh, well you're looking very well."

"Thanks."

"And your friend" he pointed to mum, who was choosing between a carton of orange juice and an iced tea, "which ward is she from?"

"Neurology," said dad, puzzled.

"Oh, she looks very well too."

"Yes, she's fine."

"So, you met here, in the hospital?" he winked.

"No, we're married, to each other, she's my wife." Dad held up his hand to show his wedding ring.

"Oh, ok." It was the guard's turn to be confused, and there was just a hint of disbelief on his face.

Their stay was going to be longer than expected, so to save on trips to the laundrette, mum decided to go shopping for clothes for her, and spare pyjamas for dad. Maria knew just the place. There was a metro stop outside the shopping centre, and they caught a train into the centre of Porto. Maria led the way.

"I had the same problem when Zé had his operation, they need a lot of changes, he's never had so many pyjamas."

"I know, I didn't think about it really, but wearing them every day means changing them like normal clothes."

"Exactly, and it's so hot in there, sometimes it's good to have short sleeves and trousers." She stopped abruptly. "Here we are. One of the nurses told me where to come, they have a big choice."

Mum looked at the shop window, it was full of nightwear. Slippers, dressing gowns, and yes, pyjamas. Maria was inside now, chatting away to the shop assistant like an old friend.

"Come, Ellen, here," she waved her arm, beckoning to mum.

It was obvious that she had recounted the whole story of dad's surgery and hospital stay. The assistant was already pulling a small step ladder out from a cupboard and leaning it against the wall. Maria shouted instructions, explaining to mum,

"Your John, I think he's taller than Zé, a little broader," she pulled herself up to her full height of about 5 feet nothing, and drew her shoulders back, to give the assistant an idea of the size they were looking for.

"Yes, I think he is," mum stifled a giggle. "I think a Large size?"

The assistant pulled out several cardboard boxes and stepped back down onto the floor.

"We have these," she opened one box and held up a traditional striped pyjama shirt, "in blue or brown or grey. And these," displaying a t-shirt and shorts set, "in blue, green, red and black." Another box, "similar to the first, but short sleeves…"

Maria was holding the tops up in rotation for mum's

approval, while the assistant climbed up for more boxes.

"These are warmer," she presented a checked jacket in a brushed cotton and reeled off the colour options. Mum was quite overwhelmed by the options available.

"I'll take a pair of the short sleeves, and one of the warmer pairs for when he's allowed outside, and one of the first type, all in blue, he likes blue."

Each pair was folded carefully and wrapped in a separate piece of colourful paper, then slotted into a large plastic bag. They had spent most of the morning there, and the whole lot came to just over thirty euros.

Finally, the neurology team decided dad was well enough to go home and they had to face the long journey back by train. Nick was away on a work trip, and I was on virtual bed rest before my operation, so we were no help. Lynne had been keeping in touch with mum by phone and text message, and happened to call as they were trying to work out a plan.

"I'll come and give you a hand."

"Are you sure? It's a long journey, about 6 hours each way."

"Aye, no bother, I've never been to Porto."

"You could come up the day before, and stay in the hotel, we'll cover all the costs."

"No, I'll just get the early train up, it gets in at lunchtime. And then there's one back in the afternoon."

"Lynne, you can't do it in one day, you'd have to be up at 6 in the morning, and not back until 9.30 at night, and spend 12 hours sitting on a train."

"It'll be a wee break for me, not having to think about curtains and deadlines, I'll enjoy it."

She was determined to go so Mum booked her a return ticket, emailed it to her, and off she went. There was just time for a quick catch up before the taxi arrived to take them back to the station. The hospital had insisted they take a folding wheelchair with them, just in case, so Mum had requested a car big enough to take the chair plus all their luggage, and extra pyjamas. However, the driver made one attempt to get it all in, then shook his head and said there wasn't enough space. It was too late to wait for another car, and if they missed the train, they would have to spend the night in Porto.

"It will all go in," said Lynne, passing the chair to the driver to hold, while she removed the arm and foot rests. "There we go," she took the chair off him and slid it into the car, piled the bags and suitcases around it, then slammed the door shut. "Come on, let's get on our way."

Once again, one of our cats was missing. The one that I worried about most, my one-eyed Camões. Despite his disability, he was most definitely an outdoor cat. If we tried to keep him inside, he literally climbed the walls and scratched at the windows and doors, howling and squealing. Every time he jumped over the fence I wondered if he would be back, and every time he did, until one day he didn't. I cried for days; he had survived so much, but somehow something had overcome him. I thought about him for weeks, and months, if I could just have known what had happened to him.

11

2009, Back surgery

At the beginning of the year, I underwent spinal fusion surgery in Lisbon. After our lovely taxi driver brought us home, I spent the next few days on complete bed rest, but my discharge notes instructed me to have the remaining staples removed on the following Monday. We planned to go to the local health centre in Lagoa, expecting that they would be able to remove them, so I got up and showered carefully, trying to keep my dressing dry, then got dressed. Just carrying out these simple tasks completely floored me and I burst into tears. I couldn't even think about getting into the car, and back out to wait in a queue at a busy clinic. I crawled back into bed and instantly fell asleep, while Nick went out to make an appointment.

The Health Centre couldn't help and directed him to the Barlavento Hospital in Portimão, but that was twice as far as Lagoa. He came back into Carvoeiro and popped in to see our GP at the time, Dr Vieira, who also didn't have the right equipment. Last stop was at the surgery at Monte Carvoeiro, where a new doctor had recently set up a private practice. Dr Habeck listened while Nick explained for the third time that morning.

"Yes, I can do that, shall I come to the house, would that be better?"

"That would be fantastic, Karen is really struggling to walk far, so if you can come out and do it, that would be absolutely wonderful."

"Ok, I will come this evening after I finish my appointments here."

Nick gave him directions, we were only a few minutes away, and he came back to deliver the good news. I couldn't believe it, once again someone we didn't know was going out of their way to make my life easier. I cried again, but this time from relief.

Nick has been in charge of almost all the cooking in our house for years, ever since, as fairly recent newlyweds, he came home from work one day and said that he didn't feel like eating the meal I had planned.

"Ok, you had better do it yourself then," I said, and he did and continues to do so.

He had just put a chicken in the oven for our dinner when Dr Habeck called to say he was leaving the surgery. I knew he would be here very quickly, and was trying to tidy myself up a bit, when I heard the gate click and Nick's voice welcoming him in. They both appeared in the doorway, Dr Habeck holding a small box, and some disinfectant and dressings.

"Hello, I hear you have been through a big surgery, how are you now?"

"It's painful when I'm standing, and I haven't been able to sit down properly yet, but I'm ok when I'm lying down."

Little did I know I would still be saying that twelve, thirteen years later, and for the rest of my life.

"Well, it's very early days, you need to rest and let your back heal, there is a lot of trauma in this type of surgery, but let me look at the staples and see what I can do."

I rolled onto my side and then onto my front with difficulty. Nick lifted my nightie and I heard a sharp intake of breath.

"Oh, I didn't expect such a big scar," he said as he peeled the dressing off. "But it has been very well done, and the skin is healing nicely, I think the rest of the staples can come out."

I suddenly felt as if they were all that was holding me together and was beginning to regret my keenness to call him in.

"Are you sure, or should we wait a few days?"

He gave a slight chuckle, "I think I can say it is ok."

"Ok."

I heard the box opening, and a clicking sound, then Nick said,

"Ah, is that what you use, can I have a look?" and they proceeded to have a chat about the tool and the process while I lay forgotten in front of them.

"Let me show you," I heard as both of them leant over me, one on each side. Don't mind me, I thought.

To be fair, I didn't feel a thing until the cold antiseptic lotion slid down my back. Nick and Dr Habeck congratulated each other on the smoothness of the procedure, as I struggled to replace my clothing.

"Oh sorry, let me do that."

I was back in the room with them. I rolled onto my back and thanked him for coming out so late.

"Not at all, I'm pleased to help. Here is my card, if you need anything, any time just let me know. My mobile number is on the back if it's an emergency."

Nick led him out through the kitchen, their conversation now turned to food.

"That smells good, what are you having tonight?"

"It's just a roast chicken."

"Well, it smells delicious, enjoy it."

I started physiotherapy again with Alison, and she recommended Pilates lessons with Debbie, a local fitness trainer and Pilates' teacher. It was important to strengthen my core, to support the rods as my spine healed. One of the side effects of the surgery is that I have much less control of my abdominal muscles than before, as the corresponding muscles in my back are virtually paralysed, along with my spine. I felt very vulnerable and it was several months before I had the confidence to leave the house but I was still expecting to make a near-full recovery and was treating this period of rehabilitation as a temporary blip.

It came as a very gradual realisation that I was not going to progress beyond a certain point. My pain felt different but not less than before. My back would go into a spasm if I did too much, walked too far, sat too long, and the only relief I got was from lying down with an ice pack, to reduce the inflammation. My lower back was permanently warm and extremely sensitive to touch, I also had a permanent 'fizzing' feeling in both feet, all due to nerve damage.

As the weeks went on, I had a curious feeling of my muscles and organs moving and sliding into place. I realised I could breathe deeply now that my lungs were no longer squashed by my spine. I had always assumed my breathlessness was due to my lack of fitness.

My first few outings were very short, fifteen minutes in the car, then a ten-minute walk, then half an hour sitting on the terrace of a café. Each trip was exhausting and I would come home and sleep for hours. I quickly found that sitting at lunchtime with a coffee or water was much more painful than sitting in the evening with a glass of wine. I had stopped all my painkillers as the milder ones did nothing, while stronger medication knocked me out. At one point I was prescribed a muscle relaxant and told to take 3 per day. After the first one at 8.30 one morning, I fell asleep until 3 in the afternoon, when I should have taken the second tablet. I woke up slurring my words and unable to focus, as if I'd had several bottles of wine, so I disposed of the rest of the packet. A glass of wine, or two, however, had just enough of a relaxant effect to allow me to sit a little longer, and a gin and tonic was even better.

Nick came home from work one day in the summer and announced,

"I've just passed a little kitten sitting on the side of the road. I stopped to try to catch it but it disappeared into a fig tree."

"Is it really tiny?"

"Yes, about 6 weeks, I think. It's right on the edge of the main road just after Intermarché. It's going to get run over, you know how fast that bit of road is."

"Do you think we can catch it?"

"I'd like to try."

It was only about six months since my spinal surgery, but off we went anyway, with a cat box and tin of tuna. I felt I should be getting back to normal, and tried to carry on as I had before the operation. We found the kitten easily; it hadn't moved far from where Nick had seen it earlier but it was extremely nervous and stayed deep within the foliage of the tree. Dishes of food had been placed nearby, so someone was looking out for it, but it was in a really dangerous situation. So many cars whizzed past as we crouched at the side of the road. I have no idea what passing drivers thought we were doing. We tried to entice it into a cat box but it stayed just out of reach. It's amazing how these stray cats and kittens seem to be able to calculate an arm's length and remain just that little bit further away. It was getting dark so we had to leave it for now.

We went back the next evening, but the kitten resolutely ignored us and any titbits we offered. On the third evening, we saw a whole fish, head, skin and skeleton had been left there; it was about three times its size and it just wasn't hungry enough.

Next to the fig tree was a small car park and an office, Nick popped in to ask about the kitten.

"Oh yes," replied the woman behind the desk, "we've been leaving food for it, it's a cute little thing, but very timid."

"My wife and I are trying to catch it, so if you could stop feeding it for a few days, it would make it easier. We will come every evening with food, so you don't need to worry."

"Ah ok," she replied. "We don't open at the weekends, so it will be hungrier then, I should think. Good luck."

We went back for the next few evenings, hoping the kitten would start to recognise and trust us, but we were no closer to catching it. It would sit peering out at us from behind the huge fig leaves, watching us intently. Any attempt to move closer resulted in it retreating out of sight, to where it felt safe. It was so pretty with beautiful big eyes and delicate black and white markings, I decided it must be a female.

The weekend was approaching so we decided to make a final serious attempt to catch her on Sunday morning. If she hadn't been fed on Saturday, she might just be hungry enough, and the road would be a bit quieter. I was worried that one wrong move on our part would send her running across the busy road.

We turned up and arranged our very unsophisticated trap. A normal cat carrier with a piece of string tied to the door and fed back through the box and out the slits in the side. We sat the box on a flat, steady surface, and Nick held it in place with his foot. I placed a trail of tinned tuna and sardines from just in front of the tree up to the entrance of the box and then right at the back. Just small pieces, hopefully not enough to fill her up before she got into the box.

We took up our positions, as far away from the box as possible, while still able to see inside and hold onto the string. All the time the big saucer eyes watched us going back and forth. Now we were ready, we stood stock still, in silence. The minutes ticked by and the sun started to burn into the back of my neck, but I didn't dare move. The kitten caught the scent of the food and her nose started to twitch. She slid out under the fig leaf and stretched her neck out to reach the first piece of food. She took it slowly then darted back to her haven.

We exchanged a look and I shrugged my shoulders, we had to give her more time. She came back out and took the next morsel, but this time she stayed out and took another step forward and another bite. Clearly, she was hungry enough and the lure of the fish was stronger than her fear. Another step and she was at the entrance to the box, she now had to decide whether to keep going or run back. We held our breath. She looked around, unsure, then put one paw inside the box, then another. Once the third paw was in, I pulled on the string, closing the door behind her. Immediately, Nick bent down and held the door shut with one hand while locking it in place with the other. She was in, and safe.

There's always a moment when I can't quite believe that we have succeeded. It's such a delicate operation and can go wrong in so many ways, but when it goes right it's so satisfying. Back home we transferred her into a cage we had prepared with everything she needed and left her to get used to her new surroundings. She really was a beautiful kitten. First thing on Monday morning we took her to the clinic for a check-up, and flea and worm treatment. And to find out that she was, in fact, a he, so we named him Figo, after his first home.

A few months later, we were taking the dogs on their evening walk when we noticed another young kitten sitting on top of the bank of post boxes next to our house. It quickly jumped down and ran into a neighbour's garden. We knew the house was empty, as the owners rarely visited from Lisbon, and also that the gate was never locked. We took the dogs home and armed with our cat box and string invention we embarked on another kitten catching expedition. At least this one was close to home.

We let ourselves into the garden and set up our trap. This kitten must have been on its own for a few days, it was definitely hungry and didn't need too much persuasion to go into the box. However, it was still close to midnight before our objective was achieved. This one was a brown and cream, almost Siamese-looking kitten. At the subsequent check-up we found out she was a girl, and we named her Honey. As they were so close in age, Figo and Honey grew up together, as close as brother and sister, and still sleep cuddled in together now. Figo still doesn't trust Nick and hisses at him if he gets too close. He's not one bit grateful to his saviour, but he does sneak up beside me in the evening, for a cuddle.

Honey and Figo

Honey and Figo did provide us with a bit of a conundrum though. When they were old enough, and both spayed/neutered, neither of them ever wanted to go out. We had become used to leaving the internal doors open and letting the cats have access to the garden via a cat flap in the kitchen door, but these two were nervous of the outside world, and usually retreated behind and under the furniture, where they felt safe. On the rare occasion that they did venture out, they panicked and leapt over the fence, with no regard for passing traffic. The situation was nerve-wracking, especially as we had lost so many, either killed on the road or just disappeared, never to be seen again. Minnie, Polly, then Cindy, Ginger and Camões, had all gone, and I dreaded losing any more.

Nick came up with a solution, once again. He planned to build a large cat cage next to the living room with access from the French doors. It was an area of the garden that we didn't really use, tucked away in a corner between the front fence and the hibiscus hedge.

Catio

The cage was more like an aviary, about seven feet high by ten feet long and made of metal fence panels, powder-coated in white. He covered half of the roof for shade and protection from the rain, but left the other half open for sunbathing, and kitted it out with a shelving system with beds on different levels, scratching posts, and even a rope ladder for the adventurers. The outside cats still went out, but most of them decided to stay within the 'catio', enjoying the fresh air and watching the birds fly past, but keeping both cats and birds safe, it was the perfect solution.

Another day, another sofa delivery, the address was a townhouse in Ferragudo. Nick followed the directions and was met by an English couple who explained they were friends of the owner.

"He works all over the world, so he asked us to help out with furnishing this place."

"Ah ok, do you live nearby?"

"We have a place just past Praia Grande, we spend quite a lot of time there, but we go back to the UK too, we split our time really."

The place was a new build and needed everything apart from the sofa he had just delivered.

"I don't suppose you know anyone who could make some curtains, do you?"

"I do as it happens, she's called Lynne and she has a workshop just down the road, shall I get her to call you."

"Oh, that would be great, thanks."

"I put the curtain poles up for her, so I know her well, she does a lovely job."

"Oh, do you think you could have a look at a few little DIY jobs here?"

"I'll have a look, certainly."

"Thanks, I'm Cliff and this is my wife, Sue, I think we'll be able to keep you busy here for a while."

In the autumn I went to see my neurosurgeon, Theo, for a check-up. He was very brisk and business-like as usual. He examined the recent x-rays that I had been instructed to have taken, murmuring to himself, then turned his attention to me.

"So how are you feeling, much better?"

"No, not really, it's still very painful," I replied.

He stared at me, quite indignant that I wasn't agreeing with him.

"You know, I didn't operate to take away your pain, I operated to stabilise your spine. You are on your own feet, so the surgery was a success, you can walk. Come back in twelve months."

We were dismissed.

One of the most frequent questions I am asked is,

'So did the operation not work?' I have to explain that it did and this is the best outcome he could have expected, he just didn't tell me at the time.

12

2010, Family visits

My brother, Steven, had just celebrated a significant birthday. We clubbed together with the rest of the family and offered to take him to Lisbon for a few days. He was delighted and booked a ten-day trip so he could spend a few days with mum and dad too. We took the train and booked the same hotel that Nick had stayed in, while I was in hospital. We planned to revisit some of the places that we had enjoyed on our first trip to the city, especially the Italian and Fado restaurants. On the first evening, we came back to the hotel bar for a nightcap. Nick got the drinks in and ordered a Jameson whiskey for Steven, knowing it was one of his favourites.

The next morning I left Nick to organise tickets for the guided tour. As I wasn't able to sit on a bumpy bus for hours now, I was quite happy to rest up and catch up on emails. After dinner that evening, we came back to the hotel bar again. This time Steven went to order a round. He came back with a tray containing a glass of wine for me, a port for Nick, and what appeared to be a half-pint of whiskey.

"What have you got there?" I asked.

He looked a bit sheepish. "I forgot about the size of the measures here," he replied. "I thought Nick had got me a double last night, so I ordered another one, but it's more like a double-double!"

I burst out laughing, "Oh, that's a good excuse, I'll have to

99

remember that one."

Despite a bit of a headache the next morning, they managed another day of sightseeing, then we started to pack for our journey back the following day. We didn't have any more nightcaps.

It was lucky that Steven had come over in February as a few weeks later, the Icelandic volcano, Eyiafjallajokul, erupted sending volcanic ash across most of Europe, causing chaos for air travellers. Flights were cancelled and no one could travel by air for weeks. I had several groups of clients stranded in their apartments, unable to leave, and other families who couldn't get here. There were daily emails to insurance companies and airlines, but until it was deemed safe to fly, we were all in limbo.

I was fortunate that none of my arriving clients was driving down, and therefore there was no pressure on the current guests to leave, but for other rental agents, it was more complicated. I received several requests for help every day and along with my owners, we did what we could to help those stranded and homeless.

Nick was also getting daily calls from people asking if he was travelling to England, and could they hitch a ride, but he had no ferry crossings booked. When the crisis was finally over, there was such a backlog that the demand for flights was overwhelming and it took several weeks to get people and planes back where they should be.

Nick's phone rang with a number that he'd stored as FrrgdoTHouse.

"Hello, it's Cliff, from the house at Ferragudo."

"Yes, I remember, nice to hear from you. What can I do for

you?"

"We've got a few things to move to our house in England, could you pop round for a chat?"

"Sure, tomorrow afternoon, ok?"

The villa was set on a slight hill, in a beautiful location, overlooking the sea. Nick could see Cliff waiting for him by the front door.

"What a great view."

"Yes, we like it," smiled Cliff. "Come in, Sue's around somewhere, can I get you a drink? Water, coffee, beer?"

"Coffee please, I've got another couple of visits this afternoon. So, what can I help you with?"

"It's an old Portuguese chest of drawers, it's in the living room here but we were thinking it would go well in our place in England. What's the best way to go about it?"

"There are a few companies I work with, I can get you a price, and if you want to go ahead, I could drop it at the depot for you."

Sue popped her head round the corner. "I thought I heard voices. Hi Nick, nice to see you again."

"Hi."

"I was just telling Nick about that piece of furniture. He's going to get a price and sort it out for us."

"Thanks, I've been meaning to get it moved but wasn't sure who to contact."

"No problem, I'll be in touch."

As Nick left, he noticed two cats sleeping in the sun.

"You've got some visitors," he remarked.

"Oh yes," said Sue, "we have quite a few, we leave a supply of biscuits out for them when we're away, and the maid keeps it topped up. We love cats, we've got three at home as well. Cliff is coming back on his own soon, we've got a proper trap and plan to catch and neuter as many as we can."

"I don't know how many we've got, I've lost count."

Nick's mum arrived on one of her regular visits, but this was to be a special one, it was her 80th birthday. She loved the food and the service at Bella Vita, the Italian restaurant on Clube Atlântico, and decided that was where she wanted to celebrate her 80th birthday, insisting that the meal was to be her treat. We booked a table for the seven of us, Nick's two brothers and partners, Nick and I, and Elsie. We had a lovely meal as usual, with all the food and drink we could manage, ending with the restaurant's signature dessert, a plate of several different miniature puddings, homemade ice cream and fresh fruit, absolutely delicious.

After coffee and limoncello, it was time to settle up, so Nick asked for the bill. Elsie once again refused all offers of payment and opened her handbag.

"Here's some cash, Nick,' she said quietly. "I'm not sure how much the bill will be but can you deal with it for me? And leave a good tip, you know, like your Dad always did."

Nick took the bundle of notes and started counting discreetly, under the table. I noticed him frown and look at his mum, she shushed him and he started counting again. He nudged me,

"Do you know how much is here?"

I shrugged; I had no idea.

"900 euros, she's been walking around with 900 euros in cash!" He was horrified.

Elsie overheard and interrupted him, "Well I wanted to make sure I had enough," she explained, "I just took a few hundred out every time I passed the cash machine."

"What did you think we were going to order?"

"I didn't know, I just wanted us all to have a lovely evening, without thinking about the cost, and we have." She was totally unrepentant.

Nick paid and returned more than half of the money to her.

"Please put that in the safe when you get back."

"Yes dear," she smiled, indulging him.

As usual, the chef waited by the front door to shake hands as we left.

We all murmured 'Grazie' and 'molto bene' as we filed past, and started putting on our coats. Elsie was still chatting to the chef, in what she remembered of the Italian she had learnt many years before. Finally, she joined us outside by the car and sat back contentedly.

"Well, that was just super, a great evening."

"Yes, it was lovely, thank you."

"You know, I just had a chat with the chef."

"Yes, we noticed, what were you talking about?"

She gave a little giggle, "Do you know, I'm not entirely sure. I either told him that Fred worked in Italy for years, or that he had a laundrette. The words are very similar and I'm not entirely sure which one I used."

We never did find out.

Another trip to the vet, another kitten brought home. Shokoley had been found on the streets of Silves and taken in by Maria José who ran a veterinary clinic in the town, and was a colleague of Filipa's. They took turns looking after her and she had become a really affectionate cat. We had gone a whole year without any additions to our four-legged family, so we volunteered to have her, and named her Amber.

A couple of months later Steve and Linda were back, staying in a large villa nearby, with many of the honeymoon guests. It wasn't one of my rental properties this time, so I was surprised to see his number flash up on my phone.

"Hi Karen, Steve here, how are you?"

"I'm fine thanks, how is your villa?"

"Oh, it's great thanks, maybe not as well equipped as the apartments, but it's nice having our own pool."

"That's good, I'm glad you're enjoying it."

"Erm, I wanted a bit of advice really. You see there's this…"

I was waiting for it…

"…kitten."

Bingo.

"Yes?"

"We saw it across the lane yesterday, but it ran away, but then this afternoon it came back. I think it must be hungry because it came a bit closer. We threw it some chicken from the BBQ, and it grabbed it and ran under a bush in the garden. It's still there now, and we go home on Saturday."

"Nick, cat box."

He was a pretty little thing, mostly white but with some silver tabby stripes on his legs and back. We took him up to Filipa, who had now taken over from her father, for a check-up. She confirmed he was a boy, but could only find one testicle. We decided to call him Womble (or one ball!). He was a good friend for Amber, and they played well together. A few weeks later I got another call, this time from mum,

"Your dad just took the girls out for a walk, and there's a kitten sheltering under the car. He says it's really small. He brought the dogs back and we're going to try and find it; if we get it, can we bring it to you? I know you've got kitten food for Womble, and we're going up to Porto for your dad's check-up next week."

"Nick…"

An hour later they arrived, carrying the new baby. The kitten was really tiny, it looked as if its eyes were just opening, and its back legs weren't fully functioning yet.

"Gosh, I knew you said it was small, but it must be only about three weeks old. Poor little thing, I wonder where his mum and siblings are?"

"We had a good look around, but couldn't see any others. This wee one was dragging himself towards us though, he knew he needed help."

He had been found at Monte Dourado, so we called him Monty. We put him down beside Womble, who was only about twelve weeks old, but he looked huge in comparison to little Monty. I bottle fed him to start with, which he loved, and he soon started to grab the bottle with his front paws, even though the bottle was almost as big as he was. Amber looked after him like a big sister, and the three of them cuddled in together in one bed.

13

2011, New puppy

Barney was really starting to slow down now. His back legs were getting quite stiff, and his eyes were milky with cataracts. We calculated that he must be 13 or 14, a good age for a big dog. We started to prepare ourselves for the inevitable. I don't like to wait until we lose a dog before getting another one, it always feels like I'm trying to replace the one we've lost. I'd rather take on a new pup or rescue first, so they know each other, and somehow, it's a gentler transition. I started to take more notice of Facebook posts for pups needing homes, waiting for the right one to come along.

However, there was something else to think about, Nick's impending 50th birthday. I didn't feel like throwing a big party as we had done before, even though I was now two years post-op I still didn't feel up to it. We decided on a short break not too far from home and booked the Hotel Albatroz in Cascais. It was the furthest I had travelled by car since my trip back from the hospital, cocooned on the back seat of the taxi. This time I was sitting in the front seat, like a normal person, but after an hour I started to regret it. Half an hour later I begged Nick to stop at the next service station. I didn't want a coffee or a loo break, I just wanted to lie down in the back seat.

Nick went in and got some snacks and cold drinks, and asked for some ice and a napkin. With my improvised ice pack pressed against my lower back, the pain started to dull. It was just enough to let me get back into the passenger seat and finish the journey.

We pulled up outside the hotel, and I attempted to walk across the car park to reception, but my legs had other ideas. My feet landed where they fell, I had very little control over them and leaned heavily on my walking stick. I must have looked a sight as the receptionist looked quite taken aback, and rushed us through check-in. Up to our room and I ignored the balcony and the beautiful sea view as I log-rolled onto the bed. Bliss.

After a rest, I managed to go down to the restaurant for dinner, then straight back to lie on the bed. The next morning was the same, down for breakfast then back to bed. Nick spent the morning on the beach on his own, then after lunch, he went for a walk around the town, on his own. I began to realise that I would probably never travel abroad again. Even if we could go first class with a flat bed, what would happen when we arrived? What would be the point in spending a fortune just to lie in a different bed, and without my home comforts? I managed a short stroll the next morning, but apart from that, I had only got up for meals. It was nice to have a few days away, and the hotel is beautiful, right on the beach, but it was just another reminder of how much my surgery had affected both our lives.

I told Filipa that we were thinking about getting another dog, and just a few days later she called.

"Someone just bring me three puppies, found in Sesmarias, no mum just three puppies. Do you want to see them?"

"Yes please, how old are they?"

"I think maybe six weeks, seven, not more."

"Ok, can we come tomorrow morning? Nick's working

today."

"Yes, no problem, see you tomorrow."

The puppies were huddled together, nervous and trembling. There was a beige female, who looked a bit like a Labrador pup, a black and white boy with a similar build, and a smaller light brown boy, who seemed more delicate and fragile. Nick picked him up and handed him to me, I could feel his tiny heart racing. He was so vulnerable, his head was down and he made no attempt to look at me or lick my hand, but I'm always a sucker for the underdog so he came home with us. We named him Henry. The older three soon coaxed him out of his shell, and he learned to play for the first time. Barney and Nikas were so gentle with him, despite the size difference, but Maisie was stricter and taught him some manners.

One of Nick's UK trips this year involved bringing over some items of furniture and personal belongings for a family who had been living in Dubai. Sharon and her husband Pete had rented their house out while they had been abroad, but had now decided to settle in Ferragudo. It was one of many international trips he had done, either on his own or with removal companies that he had got to know. They often called on him when there were pets involved, and he referred jobs to them if they were too big for his van. An added bonus was that he would go shopping and bring back enough British delicacies to stock a small grocer's shop. Friends would put in requests for tomato ketchup or baked beans, their favourite chocolate bars and biscuits. He was especially popular in the run-up to Christmas when he would return with tubs of Roses and Quality Street.

While he was away, I was looking after the animals and walking the dogs as usual. One morning I took Maisie out, and as we crossed the road she tripped over the edge of the pavement. She had never done that before. Then she did it again and then walked straight into a lamppost, I turned round and took her back home. I called Filipa and explained how concerned I was.

"Bring her to me now, I need to examine her."

I put her on the back seat, and she seemed dazed, looking around but not really focussing. As I waited in the clinic she stood facing into the corner of the room, staring into space. Filipa called us into the consulting room and lifted Maisie onto the table. She shone a light into her eyes, but there was no reaction.

"I don't understand it, she was fine yesterday, playing and running around as normal, then this morning she's falling and bumping into things."

"It is very strange, and she's a young dog, but it could be she has had a stroke which has affected her sight, and maybe her balance. I think we need to do some blood tests and an x-ray. It will take a few hours, leave her with me and come back around 5 o'clock."

I drove home with a feeling of foreboding, Filipa seemed concerned, I hoped it wasn't a stroke, but if not, what else could it be? I couldn't settle all afternoon, watching the clock until it was time to go back and pick her up.

"Well, it's a bit of a mystery, I don't see anything on the x-ray, some of the blood tests are a little high, but not so bad. I think we need to do a CT scan, but I don't have the machine, can you take her to the clinic in Carvoeiro? I will make the appointment and explain everything, I'll send a text with the time."

Back home, she was just the same. She was reluctant to move around the house and spent the evening under our bed. The next morning my phone beeped; the scan was booked for 11 am. I struggled to reach her in her hiding place but eventually, she shuffled close enough for me to attach a lead to her collar and walk her slowly out to the car.

The scan took about half an hour, and Claudia, the vet, said she would email the results to Filipa. We went back home to wait for news, and Maisie went back under the bed. A few hours later my phone rang,

"My dear, I have the results, and I don't know what to say, but there is nothing on the scan either."

"Oh, is that good… or bad?"

"I don't know, she obviously has a problem, but I can't make a diagnosis with no information. What we can do is give her a course of steroids, which may help, and see what happens, maybe do another scan next week? I can prepare the tablets if you want to collect them?"

"Ok, I'll come now."

I had to give a very precise amount, a quarter of a tablet twice a day. I saw an improvement almost immediately, and although she still didn't seem able to see clearly, she was brighter and more like herself. A second scan a week later was also inconclusive, but when we stopped the steroids, she went down again.

"She can't stay on steroids permanently," Filipa explained, "they do a lot of damage to other organs, but we have to find a balance."

It was difficult to see her struggle, I would rather she had a shorter life but a more comfortable one, but I had to take Filipa's advice. Barney's eyesight was getting worse too, I couldn't believe we were having to deal with two virtually blind dogs.

At the beginning of 2012, we noticed that Nikas had lost weight. It was very noticeable and happened very quickly, over just a few weeks. Another trip to the clinic, and some blood tests, showed that she was diabetic, another shock. We had one elderly boy with sight problems, one young dog with sight problems, and now a middle-aged diabetic dog. Filipa showed us how to test her blood sugar levels by pricking her ear, the way humans prick their fingers, and then calculating how much insulin to inject into the back of her neck. Being part Husky, Nikas had a thick ruff of fur there and it would be difficult to make sure we got the needle right into the skin, but we had to try.

Cliff and Sue were back in Portugal and got in touch with Nick for help with a different problem.

"There's a little black and white kitten that we've been feeding, and he's become very friendly. We're really fond of him and would like to take him back. Do you know what we'd have to do?"

"Yes, I've been taking a few animals back and forward for the last couple of years, but it's even easier now. You need to get him microchipped and vaccinated, then get a pet passport."

"Ok, that's fine, the only problem is that we are leaving next week. Is there somewhere that could look after him until he can travel?"

"I'm sure Karen wouldn't mind fostering him for you, then I could bring him over on my next trip?"

"Perfect, are you sure she won't mind?"

"I'm pretty sure she'll be ok with it," he laughed.

We arranged to meet for a meal, to finalise all the details for Ollie's stay with us. It was the first time I had met them, and we had plenty to talk about. Sue was interested in all our feline friends and grateful for our help.

"We didn't know that day when you delivered a sofa to the townhouse, that you'd end up bringing a cat over to us."

Nick picked Ollie up on their last day, and brought him back, to start getting him ready for his journey to his new home.

14

Good Neighbours

Our neighbour Ana and her husband had split up, and we heard that they had both moved out, and the house was for sale. It didn't really affect us as it was located at the end of a cul-de-sac, behind us, so we had no reason to go past it. One afternoon Nick was working in the garden, and overheard an estate agent doing a viewing,

"I think an English family is looking at Ana's house."

"I wonder if it will be to live in, or a holiday rental."

"Yes, I wonder. Anyway, we don't know whether they're going to buy it."

"No, true."

A few weeks passed, and Nick was back in the garden, this time talking on his phone. A car pulled up on the other side of the back fence, and he heard voices but carried on with his conversation. Suddenly he heard a shout,

"Nick! Is that you Nick?" It was a woman's voice.

"Hang on a minute,' he said into his phone, "someone is calling me." He went to the fence and replied, "Yes, I'm Nick, who's that?"

"It's Sharon, you know, Pete and Sharon, you brought our stuff over from England last year?"

"Oh right, I remember now, you've been in Dubai."

"Yes, that's us. Is that your house?"

"Yes, we've been here, oh about ten years now."

"Well, we're your new neighbours. We won't be moving in just yet, we're having some work done first, but I'll be in touch as we'll need some boxes moved from Ferragudo."

"No problem, just give me a call when you're ready."

We are constantly surprised by the coincidences we have come across while we have lived here. The Algarve can be a really small place.

Ollie had his pet passport and Nick planned to take him on his next trip to the U.K. He had been asked to take some personal belongings over for a client, who also wanted to bring some furniture to their house in Portugal. Ollie would travel in a large cage on the front seat, next to Nick. After landing in Portsmouth, he would deliver Ollie, then go on to his next stop a few hours away.

"Hi Cliff, I'll be with you on Tuesday to drop Ollie off, but it will probably be about tea time. Is there a hotel or B&B you can recommend me to stay in that night?"

"Yes, you can stay here," Cliff replied.

"I don't want to put you to any trouble."

"No trouble at all, we've got plenty of space, and it will be good for Ollie to have you here while he gets used to us again."

Nick stayed that night and has continued to do so many times since. Cliff and Sue have been very kind and generous hosts, and we meet up regularly in Portugal too. All down to that first sofa delivery.

It became more difficult to control Nikas's blood sugar. Her readings varied wildly and she started to lose weight again. Blood tests showed that her pancreas was failing. We were going to have to make a decision. We talked it over, trying to convince ourselves that she had a bit more time, but events overtook us and she collapsed with suspected pancreatitis, and the decision was taken out of our hands. We had to say a sad goodbye to Nikas and all her crazy escape artist adventures.

Before we had even had a chance to grieve for her properly, I noticed Monty was walking strangely, he seemed to be dragging his back legs. A few times recently, we had found a poo just outside the litter tray, and I wondered now if it was because he couldn't manage to get his bottom into it properly. I took him up to the clinic for an examination and blood tests. Filipa looked concerned when she saw him.

"You don't think he can have an injury?"

"No, not anything I know of, he's grown out of playing rough and tumble games with Womble now."

"Ok, I tell you something later, don't worry."

Too late, I was already worrying. I watched him like a hawk, he was definitely weaker and slower.

"Hello my dear, I have the test results, but it's not very good news. I think Monty have a lymphoma."

"Oh. Cancer."

"Yes, I'm so sorry."

"What can we do, is there a treatment?"

"We can try with some chemotherapy, sometimes it have a good outcome."

"Only sometimes?"

"Yes."

My poor little Monty. So cheeky and cute and loving, and so young.

Monty and Womble

Pete and Sharon finally moved in with their three younger children, the eldest was at university in England, two dogs and two cats. Nick helped as promised, not just with their belongings but also with deliveries of furniture. Once they had settled in, they invited us round for a grand tour. Sharon and I found that we had lots in common, mostly a love of animals, but also that Pete worked away a lot, so there were times when we were both on our own. We swapped numbers, happy to know that we both had someone nearby to call on in an emergency. The call came a bit quicker than we had expected.

"Karen, it's Sharon, I think Sushi has reacted to something and her mouth is swelling up. I don't suppose you've got anything I can give her?"

"I've got some anti histamines, and cortisone here, do you want to call the emergency vet and see what they say?"

I gave her the names and strengths of some of the medications I had for Barney, Monty and Maisie. Five minutes later she called back,

"They said to try the cortisone, half a tablet for her weight, is that ok?"

"Yes, no problem, I'll get it now. There's a small gap in our back fence, it's close to your gate, I'll leave it there."

The medication worked quickly and Sushi was soon back to normal, and the little gap in the fence became the easiest way for us to pass small items to each other. Some icing sugar, flour, a piece of birthday cake, a spare bulb or battery, anything either of us needs to borrow or wants to pass on.

In November we had the usual spell of blustery weather that accompanies the season changes. I was lying in bed one day when I heard a loud rumbling noise. It got louder and louder and seemed to be coming nearer, then disappeared as quickly as it came. It was like nothing I had heard before, not even an earthquake. I checked on the internet, to see if anyone else had heard it, and was astonished to see it had been a tornado. People started posting photographs, and it soon became apparent that it had started out at sea, hit land just to the west of Carvoeiro, and passed within 500 metres of our house. It continued up through Lagoa, causing quite a bit of damage to cars and buildings, and onto Silves where it destroyed part of the football stadium. It's a rare phenomenon but another example of the extremes that we can experience here.

I was back in hospital a few weeks before Christmas, this time it was for a hysterectomy. I knew it was major abdominal surgery and was prepared for a lengthy recovery, but I didn't realise just how tiring it would be. I was exhausted for the first few weeks and was back to needing help to get out of bed or to take a shower. As soon as David and Marianne heard I was convalescing, she rang Nick.

"I heard Karen has been in for another operation, how is she?"

"She's ok, but it has wiped her out a bit."

"So I gather, it's a big op, give her our love. Anyway, I rang to say we're having fish pie tonight. I'll plate up some for you two, it will be ready about 6, is that ok?"

"Don't worry about us Marianne, I can still do the cooking."

"Yes but you're working and looking after Karen, it's just as easy for me to make for four as for two. See you later." And she put the phone down.

Nick went round intending to persuade her that we were fine, but she ignored him and handed him two oval dishes, topped with mashed potato.

"Here's a dish of vegetables, and some extra sauce, now take it while it's hot and you won't need to heat it up. Pork casserole tomorrow."

He appealed to David, who just shrugged his shoulders,

"Nothing to do with me," he smiled.

Every day she cooked us something different, accompanied by side dishes of vegetables and jugs of gravy. There was no point arguing with her, so Nick started buying supplies of meat and fish as our contribution, with a few bottles of wine as a tip. Marianne carried on like this for weeks, until I was well on the way to recovery and we could say, thank you but we really are ok again. It was such a kind and selfless act, and we will always be grateful to them both.

We started Monty on his chemo tablets, and they helped to start with. But soon we had to increase the dose, and then his fur started to fall out. He was a pathetic sight, from being so strong and vital, he was barely a shadow. Filipa consulted with Maria José in Silves and Claudia in Carvoeiro, but there was no breakthrough, and we all gathered in tears, as we lost yet another precious little one.

We have lost so many, in different circumstances. Most people only have to face it maybe once every ten or twelve years, but having so many animals multiplies the joy, but also the pain. It's incredibly difficult to be the one to say 'enough' but through our experiences, I have come to feel a little stronger when the time comes. We will always be devastated, every time, but I try to see it from the animal's perspective. It must be so confusing for them when we, who have loved and fed and cared for them, suddenly start forcing tablets or needles into them. We can never know how much pain they are in, cats, in particular, are very good at masking symptoms until they become acute. I have learned that for me, I would rather make the decision a week too early than a day too late. If I can't give them a good life, then the best I can do is give them a good death. Safe, warm, cared for and as comfortable as possible. I try not to have a crisis situation, or just delay the inevitable, we do our best, but sometimes it just isn't enough.

Life goes on, and there's always another little soul out there needing rescuing. Cliff and Sue had arrived for their summer visit and found another little black and white kitten in the garden, so like Ollie that we think they probably had the same mum. We agreed to foster her and get her spayed, but as usual, she stayed. We called her Mabel. She didn't have a playmate, as the other cats were too grown up to be interested, then dad said he had been leaving food out for some kittens that were roughly the same age. The only problem was that they were in a fairly inaccessible place, the other side of a solid wall.

We went to investigate and saw four of them playing in a patch of long grass, but way out of our reach. They were quite feral too, and would only come to eat once they were left on their own. The only chance of catching them was a small drainage hole cut into the bottom of the wall, maybe we could tempt one or two of them by leaving food near the gap. We went back when we thought they would be hungry, and put a plate of sardines just far enough away that they would have to come right through, and not just stretch their heads out to grab the food and then disappear. Nick watched over the wall, as mum, dad and I waited near the food. There were a few false starts, then a little ginger head appeared, sniffing the air. He spotted the fish and took a step closer, then another. He was almost at the dish, it was now or never, dad leaned over and in one movement picked him up and handed him to me. The little one was in a cat box before he knew what was happening. We brought him home as a friend for Mabel and called him Mack.

Cliff also had some more work for Nick.

"We've got a friend who needs to sell his villa and downsize. He's 90 and had a stroke last year, and he really can't manage now. We were wondering if you could come and help empty the place?"

"Yes, of course, is there a lot of stuff to move?"

"Oh yes, some will go to his new apartment in the centre of Ferragudo, and there's some he wants to sell, but also quite a lot to be sorted out and maybe just dumped."

Nick went to meet Cliff and was introduced to Lenny, originally from New York, but resident in the Algarve for the last 40 years. Although he was now confined to a wheelchair most of the time, he didn't take any nonsense.

"Don't take anything before I've looked at it," he warned. "Some of that stuff is worth a few bucks."

Nick looked at Cliff, who just raised his eyebrows.

"Nick is here to help out, you can't do it, and I'm not going to, so you'd better be nice to him," replied Cliff.

Lenny chuckled, "Ok boss."

They actually got on well together, and Nick gave as good as he got, I think Lenny respected that. One room was full of boxes of books, most of them were old and dusty and hadn't been touched for years.

"What do you want to do with these?" asked Nick.

"I'm not giving them away, let's sell them at the next second-hand sale."

Nick often had a stall at local car boot type sales, so agreed to book a space at the next one in Ferragudo. He turned up early on a Sunday morning to find Lenny guarding their space on his mobility scooter.

"Hi Lenny, you're here early."

"Yeah, I didn't want anyone stealing our spot."

"Lenny?"

"Yeah?"

"What are you wearing?"

"I've come dressed as a monk."

"Why?"

"To attract some attention, to sell my books. Whaddaya think?"

"I think you'll get plenty of attention."

"Good."

Nick set up a table and chair and started piling up the books. Lenny picked one off the top and slid it onto the chair,

"I think I'll keep that one.'

"Lenny, we're supposed to be selling them."

"Yeah but I forgot about that one, I think I'll need it."

"Ok but just that one."

"Yeah."

Nick emptied another box full onto the table and spoke to a potential customer. He turned to ask Lenny a question and caught him hiding another book.

"Come on, we're trying to get rid of all of these, how many have you taken back?"

"Not many." Lenny stuck his lower lip out like a sulky teenager.

"There's at least a dozen on that chair. No more."

"Ok boss."

Lenny decided to show willing and started zooming up and down in front of the stall shouting,

"Books for sale, antique books for sale."

But any time someone enquired about the price of a particular volume he asked for 20€ and they walked away.

"You've got to be realistic, you'll get about a euro a book here."

"They're worth more than that."

"I warned you before we came, people look for bargains at these places, we're not at Sotheby's."

Lenny went back into a sulk.

After five hours they packed up, having sold no more than twenty books. Lenny wasn't disappointed at all, he'd had a morning out, and he still had almost all his books.

Another loss, this time Skip. Nick found him lying on the front step, his sides heaving as he struggled to breathe. He didn't resist as we put him in a box and Nick took him to the clinic.

Filipa could hear fluid on his lungs and sent them to Claudia for an urgent x-ray. Nick returned with the results; his lungs were covered in tumours. There was no possibility of treatment and he had to make the decision there and then. Goodnight sweet little Skip.

One of the advantages of the cat cage was the reduction in nocturnal cat fights. Several neighbours now had cats too, some of whom were determined to come into our garden, despite our outside cats and the dogs. Pete and Sharon had brought two dogs and two cats with them. The dogs, Sushi and Blackie had both been rescued recently, Frankie the cat had been found on the streets in Ferragudo, but Dave had come with them from Dubai. They had taken him on after he was left at the vets with a badly infected leg wound, probably from a fight. The leg had to be amputated but that only seemed to increase his confidence. He appeared regularly, walking along the top of the garden wall full of bravado.

He didn't realise that neither Barney nor Maisie could see him, and Henry was frightened of his own shadow and was never going to challenge him. Smokey, however, was a different story, this was his garden and he guarded it fiercely. We were often woken by loud yowling as they faced each other up in a standoff. We resorted to keeping a bottle of water handy to throw over them, or using the hosepipe if they were on the other side of the fence, but it only stopped them temporarily.

Dave got more and more brazen, and one Saturday morning he just wouldn't move. We tried the water trick, he just turned his back on us, we tried to shoo him away, he hissed and balanced on his hind legs to swipe at us with claws out. I had to phone Sharon.

"We've got Dave in the garden and he won't budge, can you come and get him?"

"Oh sorry, yes Pete's here, I'll send him round."

We thought it would be easy enough, Dave would see Pete and there would be a happy reunion. Dave had other ideas. As Pete approached, he went into full attack mode with an 'I don't even know who you are,' look on his face.

"I should have brought the oven gloves," said Pete.

We finally got him out by opening the gate wide, Nick and Pete encouraging him forward, and me following with the hosepipe.

Barney was still plodding on, still enjoying his food and short walks, but sleeping more, and so soundly that I sometimes had to check he was still breathing. He started to sleep through thunder and lightning, and fireworks. He could lie on the kitchen floor with us stepping over him and remain completely oblivious. Maisie was still on regular short courses of steroids, but without them, she went down quickly. She was very sensitive to touch on her head and neck and I was beginning to think she had a brain tumour. Maybe it had been too small to show up on the scan but was starting to grow now. There was definitely something very wrong.

15

2014, Rupert

Just after New Year mum saw an appeal on Facebook. A litter of pups were in a field in Lagoa, and the neighbouring farmer wanted them gone as he was worried about his chickens. Mum made contact with the person who had written the post, for directions, and Nick took her to find them. There were five of them, about seven or eight weeks old. Mum took them home with her and installed them in their spare bedroom. I couldn't wait to see them, so we went up that evening.

It was chaos with five pups and the three of us in the bedroom/study. The little ones were full of energy, jumping up on our laps and smothering us with kisses, no longer having to survive the cold January temperatures, out in the open. They were gorgeous pups, but with two dogs and five cats, mum knew they couldn't keep them permanently. The first girl went very quickly, to a couple living in the hills above Faro. The next little boy went to a family in Portimão, with a ten-year-old boy who had been desperate for a dog for years, and his parents felt he was now old enough to help take care of it.

That left two boys and a girl. One of the boys had a broad white stripe down his face and was always the first to want a cuddle from me. We now knew that we were likely to lose both Barney and Maisie soon, which would leave Henry on his own, so we took him home. We named him Rupert.

Henry had fitted in so well with the other dogs that we

assumed he would be fine with a puppy; he was still fairly young himself. This was our first mistake, Henry hated Rupert on sight.

"I'm sure he'll come round," I said, hopefully, "we'll just have to give him some time."

Rupert stayed in the living room most of the time, glad of the warmth and security, and we put a large dog crate up for him so he got some peace from the cats. Barney and Maisie rarely came into the living room now, they were either out in the garden, or in the bedroom where they didn't get disturbed, but Henry would come in, look at Rupert, and go straight back out. Maybe I was wrong, but I was determined not to give up on either of them.

As Rupert grew, we put up a stair gate between the kitchen and the hall, and fed them treats for good behaviour and 'nice kisses' any sign of aggression and we shut the door. We realised that Henry was actually terrified, he was always a nervous boy and the unpredictability of a small puppy was overwhelming him. We progressed to fencing off part of the garden and me supervising Rupert on one side, while Henry could come and say hello, but was also free to ignore him. This went on all summer. The next step was taking them out for a walk together, but apart, liberally dispensing treats as we went. By the time Rupert was a year old, we could let them into the garden together, under close supervision, but we had come a long way. The first time I saw them lying side by side on a sunbed I nearly cried with happiness.

Henry and Rupert

Nick was still helping Lenny. He persuaded him to move some boxes into a storage facility, then focus on what was going to be sold along with the villa, and what he needed in the new apartment. After a couple of trips in the van, the villa was ready to be cleaned and put on the market, and Lenny moved out.

The local council announced there would be a new event in Carvoeiro in June. To celebrate the summer solstice, they would hold a 'Black and White' night. The village would be decorated in black and white banners and balloons, and everyone attending should dress accordingly.

It was a very ambitious plan, the centre of the village would be pedestrian-only, and there would be free shuttle buses from parking areas on the outskirts. We went down early, as I'm nervous of getting jostled in large crowds, and watched as several stages were set up along the out road, and up Estrada do Farol. There was also a stage on the beach for a DJ who would play until 3 am. Every type of music was represented from Fado to Folk to Rock, and there were displays of dancing, fire-eating and Capoeira, a Brazilian martial art that incorporates dance and acrobatics. As the place filled up, we headed home, but we heard it was a great success with a crowd of around 20,000 people. Almost immediately it was announced that it would be a regular event, and visitors started booking their holidays around Black and White night.

Sharon and I were in touch regularly, especially when we were both on our own. Instead of long text conversations, we decided to go to Vila Nova, a nearby restaurant for lunch and a proper catch-up. We sat at an outside table, overlooking the swimming pool and close to the car park. As we picked up the menus, we were interrupted by an elderly Asian man holding a map. He didn't speak a lot of English, and no Portuguese, but he kept pointing at his map. Sharon took it from him and worked out that he was trying to get to an apartment in Sesmarias. She tried to draw a better map from the restaurant to his accommodation, but he looked even more confused. She stood up,

"I," she pointed to herself, "come with you," pointing to his car, and then miming turning a steering wheel.

He smiled and nodded, bowed to me, and turned away.

"I won't be long, order me the salmon," she said.

About ten minutes later she was back, just as our meals arrived. They had dropped the man's wife and luggage at reception, and he had brought her back, we just hoped that he would remember the way or this could be a very long afternoon.

Within just a few months of each other we lost first Maisie, then Barney. They had both fought for so long and tried so hard, but finally they succumbed to their different health problems. Barney must have been 17 or 18, an incredible age for a dog his size, and with his history. We lost him to a suspected stroke. Maisie was only young, but had already suffered more than many older dogs, and a combination of the growing brain tumour and the steroids used to treat it, were just too much for her.

A private message arrived on my Facebook account, it was from Steve and Maria.

'We're coming over in a few weeks, but we'd like to surprise Nick. We're staying in an apartment in Carvoeiro, can we arrange to meet you somewhere for a meal but let him think it's just going to be the two of you?'

'That's a great idea.'

'Ok, it will be the first week in December.'

'No problem. Look forward to it.'

Over the next few weeks, we made a plan. I booked a table at Oasis for their first evening and was keen to see Nick's face when he saw them.

The flight was on time and they landed about lunchtime. They stopped at Intermarche for some groceries on their way to the apartment, and as they got to the till who did they see in front of them? Nick.

He did get a surprise, but not quite the one we had planned. Never mind, we still went out for dinner and sat chatting well after we had finished eating. It was great to catch up on all their news. Maria was now studying homoeopathy and Steve was keeping busy as a Fire Safety Officer, and the kids were now almost grown-up.

"So, are you thinking of coming back permanently?"

"You never know," said Steve, with a wink.

16

2015, Wedding bells

We had owned the apartment for over 15 years, and although we had changed beds and furniture, the kitchens and bathrooms were beginning to look their age. We planned to carry out the work through the winter when bookings are quieter, so we blocked out November until March. The work took longer than we expected, and we only managed to complete the two bathrooms and downstairs cloakroom before it was Spring again. The kitchen would have to do another season.

Nick came home with another kitten he had found dumped in a box, by the edge of a field in Lagoa. It was cold and hungry, and its eyes were still closed. I found my emergency pack of kitten milk, cleaned out a bottle and got to work. She was a cute little thing, jet black but even at just a few weeks old, I could tell she was going to be a character. Mum and dad still had Beca and her kittens, although Charlie had passed away at home a few years ago. They came to see the new addition and were quite taken with her.

When she was fully weaned, they offered to take her, so she joined their four-legged friends. They named her Nora. Her personality showed itself when she was old enough to be spayed. They brought her home, post-op, wearing a recovery suit, like a leotard that zips up along the back, which meant that she didn't need to wear a lampshade collar, something she definitely wouldn't tolerate. Mum expected her to be drowsy after the anaesthetic, but she was manic, climbing her cage and hanging from the roof bars like a bat. Mum left her in the dark in the spare room, hoping she would fall asleep in the peace and quiet.

The next morning, she went in to find Nora still performing gymnastics, but without her suit. Somehow, she had managed to wriggle out of it and it lay in the corner of the cage, discarded and ignored. She seems to think she's a dog and accompanies mum when she walks her real dogs. Passers-by are forever warning her that there's a cat following behind, and to be careful if the dogs see her. They don't realise that she sleeps with them on the bed every night.

Nick got a text from Steve,

'Just to let you know, we're getting married.'

'That's great. Congratulations. When?'

'Next year. In Lagoa.'

'Really? Wow.'

An email followed with all the details. There would be a small legal ceremony in London, in December, but it would be followed by a Blessing service in Lagoa, at the Fire Station.

"I don't think I've ever heard of a wedding in a fire station," said Nick.

"Neither have I, do you think we'll have to slide down a pole?"

Nick had kept in touch with Lenny, calling in for a coffee when he was passing, but his health was deteriorating further. Cliff rang to let us know that he had been taken into hospital just before Christmas, so Nick went to visit, taking some chocolate brownies I had made. His eyes lit up when he saw them.

"The food in here is terrible, I barely eat any of it, but those brownies look good."

"Is there anything I can bring you?" Nick asked.

"Some more brownies please."

Nick didn't get a chance to take any more as Lenny died in the first week of January, 2016. He had requested a simple funeral, no church service, and no fuss. He had already arranged a 'gaveta' next to his wife in the cemetery in Ferragudo. Nick went to see him off.

The gavetas are built around the sides of the cemetery, rows of boxes with glass doors, three or four high. Individual coffins are slid into each box, and relatives place photos and mementoes of their loved ones inside. Some of Lenny's friends said a few words, then the pallbearers lifted the coffin towards the open door of the gaveta, but it wouldn't go in. They tried again, but it was too big. They called the gravedigger over, who is also in charge of maintenance in the cemetery, and he tried filing the edges of the metal frame. It still wouldn't go in. The mourners were beginning to shuffle their feet in the cold January wind. The whole metal frame was removed, while everyone watched, and with a sigh of relief from the pallbearers, they pushed Lenny into his final home. Everyone agreed it was typical Lenny, mischievous to the end.

Steve and **Maria**'s Blessing service was arranged for the beginning of February and was held in the ceremonial room on the first floor of the Station. We arrived to find the room laid out with rows of chairs on each side, and a central aisle. Guests were arriving from all directions, Portuguese, Dutch and British, as many of their friends and family had travelled from the UK. Nick was the best man and almost as nervous as Steve.

The room slowly filled up, then as music played, Maria came down the aisle. She looked beautiful in a fitted lace dress and carrying a colourful bouquet, which on closer inspection, was made from Chupa Chup lollipops.

The reception was held in the Fatacil restaurant, where they used to go for lunch when they were on duty, all those years ago, but we didn't make any chip butties. They didn't want a traditional wedding cake but had asked me to make trays of chocolate brownies, which were piled up in small pyramids and decorated with edible flowers and glitter. It was a great day and marked the start of their new life, and their move back to Portugal.

We finished work on the apartment and turned our attention to our own house. It suddenly looked very shabby and was in desperate need of a coat of paint. We engaged a team of builders who set to work, preparing the exterior walls. There are always small cracks to be filled in, due to the minor earthquakes we have virtually every day. Occasionally there's a bigger one that is noticeable, but I've only felt three of four since we moved here. In the course of their work, they found we had a few cracked roof tiles, so they were replaced. Then we noticed that the new paintwork made the shutters look faded, so we ordered new ones.

As each job was completed, we looked more critically at other parts of the house. Nick was due to leave on a work trip, and I was left to supervise the builders and plan the next stage of the refurbishment.

Late one evening I scrolled through Facebook before going to sleep. I was shattered, but I liked to check for any local news, last thing at night. A post caught my eye,

'I've just rescued two abandoned kittens, probably a day old, still with their umbilical cords attached. Can anyone help, I don't know anything about hand-rearing kittens.'

I sent a private message straight away.

'Where are you? I'm near Lagoa and have bottle fed lots of pups and kittens.'

Almost immediately my phone pinged with a reply.

'Near Guia, can you send your number and I'll call you?'

I sent my number and it rang almost immediately. I could hear the pitiful cries of hungry kittens in the background.

"Hi. I'm Diana, I'm so glad you saw the message, I didn't think anyone would reply at this time."

"I was just going to bed but I'm happy to take the kittens if there's no one else."

"Would you, please? That would be fantastic. Can we bring them to you now?"

"Erm yes, of course, I'll get some milk ready."

I looked at my phone, it was just after 11 pm. I sent another message with the address and directions and got up to dig out some kitten formula and a bottle. I knew they would be tiny so a cat carrier was the best place for them. Even though it was a warm night they were still at risk of hypothermia, so I lined the box with warm fleece blankets while I waited for the kettle to boil. The phone rang again.

"We're in Lagoa, at the main roundabout, can you direct us in?"

I stayed on the phone until I knew they were almost at the

door. By the time they pulled up outside I was waiting at the gate. Diana got out of the car carrying a shoebox lined with a tartan blanket. I heard the crying before I saw the two little kittens, snuggled together. Their fur was sticky, their poor mum hadn't even been given the chance to lick them clean. I made sure Diana knew how to get back to the main road, then took the babies inside. The milk was still warm, but not too hot that it could hurt them. One at a time I held them and tried to feed them, but they were cold and reluctant to take the bottle. I let them snuggle together in the cat box for a few minutes, covered with a blanket. Time to try a syringe, just to let them get the taste and enough strength to suck at the bottle. I carefully managed to get them to take about 10ml each, then held some tissue in one hand and massaged them until they emptied their tiny bladders.

The crying stopped and they settled quickly, calm now and breathing more regularly. I fed them every hour that night, and by the morning they felt more solid and were able to take the bottle of milk. Sadly, one of the kittens didn't make it past the second day, but the other, who we named Doris, grew stronger and survived. We kept her, and still have her today. She's a character, quite bossy sometimes, but also very affectionate. I'm sure she remembers that I was the one who spent all those hours with her, willing her through. She's also one of the greediest cats we've ever had, I think somewhere deep down she remembers being cold and hungry and alone.

Nick came back, unsurprised to see the new addition, and ready to plough on with the renovations. The kitchen was twelve years old, and although the cabinets were sturdy, the doors hadn't aged well, so we had those replaced, and changed the layout slightly. I had never been keen on the floor tiles but the new, light kitchen made the dark, dull terracotta look even worse. It would be a huge job to re-tile the kitchen, hall, bedroom and living room but we had been living in chaos for weeks now, and if we stopped, I doubted that we would ever start again.

If we were going to do the living room floor, now was the time to think about removing the dividing wall. We knew we could take it down, as it had previously only been waist high when it formed part of the reception desk, and it was Tom who had built it up to the ceiling, to create a small bedroom. When we moved in it was a useful office space, but now I used my phone and iPad rather than a desktop computer and fax machine. We discussed it with the builders, it was now or never.

Nick returned from doing a job in Vilamoura for a rental/management/real estate company. They had used him many times over the years when a property needed to be kitted out for rentals, or was being sold and had to be emptied. This was the case for the apartment he had just left, not only had it been sold, but the owners also had a car that they wanted to sell. It had been stored in an underground garage and only used a handful of times on their visits from the UK and they had no need for it now. He excitedly took out his phone to show me photos, but they were so dark I could barely make out that it was actually a car, never mind the make or colour.

"So, what is it?" I asked, turning the phone round to try to make sense of the images.

"It's a Saab, convertible, electric blue. It's a beauty."

"Oh, is it? Do you know someone that wants one?"

"Yes, me."

"You? Why do you want a car, you've got the van for work and we've got my car for everything else?"

"But this is different, it's a bit special, and as it's still on UK plates, it's a good price too."

"No, no, no. You know what matriculating a car means. It's difficult and expensive and takes forever. Do we need that hassle on top of living in a building site?"

"Not if you pay the tax."

"Did you hear the expensive bit?" I queried.

"I made a few calls…"

"Already? But you've only just seen it."

"Yes, well I wanted to see if it was even a possibility, and I think it is."

"Ok, go on."

"Because the owner is selling it at a lower price, because of the matriculation issue, and because of the age of the car, the tax plus the purchase price is still a bargain."

"And the paperwork?"

"We'll get someone to sort that out like when we got our residência, you remember, what was her name again?"

"So, you've got it all planned out?"

"Yes, more or less, just think, driving around with the top down in summer. And actually, that's one of the best things, because it's a convertible, you'll be able to get into it easily," he finished triumphantly, knowing I couldn't argue with that.

"Ok, what's next, have you driven it?"

"Not yet, it hasn't been used for ages so the battery was flat, but I'll go back next week and have a better look and a test drive."

The car was in immaculate condition with very low mileage, Nick couldn't resist. It arrived on a low-loader and stayed on the drive while we got the matriculation process underway. I had to admit it was a striking colour and shape, and the seats were actually really comfortable.

The wall came down. The difference was amazing, we had so much more space, and finally, some straight walls. There were some small problems, such as the phone cable being built into the wall, but it was relocated next to the front door. As the rubble was cleared away, and the tiler prepared the floor we found another, more significant issue. We assumed the wall had been built on top of the floor. Wrong. The wall had been built first, then the floor laid either side, and they weren't the same height. It wasn't enough of a difference to create a step, but there was going to be a definite slope. The tiler did what he could to smooth it out, and we figured that furniture would hide the worst of it, but it can still catch me off guard occasionally.

We finally got the Portuguese number plates for the Saab and Nick was eager to take our first trip round the village.

"You know this is the start of your mid-life crisis?"

"Yep, but it's fun."

I had to agree.

The ceiling and walls had to be re-plastered, which meant the room had to be painted, and then they might as well do the rest of the house while they were here. We started off with painting the exterior in May, and finished with painting the interior in

December, having changed almost everything in between.

After twenty years of living with Parkinson's Disease, dad died peacefully in hospital, with mum and Anne-Marie at his bedside. After such a long time, we thought we were prepared, but it still came as a shock. We had attended several funerals but had no idea of the process of reporting a death or arranging a funeral. A Portuguese friend had used a company in Lagoa, so I suggested to mum that we should go and talk to them, and find out how to negotiate this new situation. A young woman sat behind the desk, I stepped forward and voiced for the first time,

"O meu pai morreu." (my father has died)

Her eyes filled up as she pulled a piece of paper from a drawer, and motioned for us to sit. Nick and Anne-Marie had come with us to help make decisions. She introduced herself as Fatima and asked for mum and dad's residência cards. After taking down the details, she returned mum's but explained she would need to keep dad's,

"We will need identification when we collect him from the hospital, and also to register the death."

"Oh, we don't have to do that?"

"No, we take care of everything, don't worry."

Her manner was gentle and reassuring, but efficient too. We felt we were in good hands. We chose the coffin and floral tributes, and she said she would contact an English-speaking priest to conduct the service.

"Is tomorrow ok for you?"

"Does it have to be tomorrow?" We knew funerals happened quickly here, but we had family travelling over.

"No, it doesn't have to be, it is traditional but we can wait. Friday?"

"Yes, that should be ok."

"On Thursday evening the coffin will be taken into the chapel, across the street, and you can spend as long as you want there."

"Can we play music?" I asked.

"Yes, some songs or pieces of music, it doesn't have to be religious."

I started thinking about making a playlist of some of dad's favourites. Fatima made a note of all our requests and calculated the cost, it was much less than we had expected.

"Do you want payment now?" I assumed we would have to pay a deposit at least.

"No, no,' she waved the suggestion away, "not yet, later."

Everything went according to plan, she delivered the death certificate and ordered additional copies, arranged for it to be translated so mum could notify their UK bank and government agencies. She took away a lot of the stress of that very difficult time.

At the vigil on Thursday evening, we were left alone in the chapel for two hours, with just our private thoughts as a family, and my playlist in the background.

As we left, the key holder was waiting to lock up. She was a small Portuguese woman, in her 70s at a guess. She must live nearby as she had come out in her slippers, not realising it was raining heavily. She was very kind and patted us on the arm as we filed out. We had booked taxis to take us to one of dad's favourite restaurants, and sheltered under a shop awning while we waited for them to arrive. When she saw us huddled together, she went back inside the chapel and brought out an umbrella. She crossed the square and waited, holding the umbrella over us as an extension to the awning. Several times I suggested she went home, out of the cold and rain, but she wouldn't leave until our taxis came. Another small but meaningful kindness.

The next morning, we were back at 11 am, joined by Steve in his Fire Service uniform, Lynne, Sharon, David and Marianne and Jan from the kennels, amongst others. The centre of Lagoa was being dug up for a new drainage system, and the roads were chaos. We left in the hearse, with mourners walking behind. A car of the Guarda Nacional Republicana, or National Guard, led the procession as we were forced to go the wrong way around the one-way system. Dad would have enjoyed that.

At the cemetery, we stood at the graveside and watched as a rainbow appeared, directly overhead. Dad was always happy in Portugal, whether on holiday or living here, and Portugal treated him very well. He never wanted to leave, and now he never will.

17

2017, Fat Cat

Womble seemed a bit lethargic and not his usual bouncy self. It happened very quickly, as is so often the case with cats, and after blood tests and an x-ray we found out that he also had numerous tumours in his lungs. Another sad goodbye, but we were glad that he had come home and not faded away under a bush somewhere. With all our waifs and strays, if we hadn't taken them in, they would have had a much shorter and more stressful life. We do what we can for them, while we can.

We were having dinner one evening on the terrace at Jomar, on the in road, when we noticed a little grey tabby kitten scavenging for scraps under the table. We asked Miguel, the waiter and son of the owners about it.

"Yes, we know, it comes sometimes, but runs away very quickly."

I was concerned about it being so close to the road and suggested we borrow the cat trap from Cliff and Sue and set it up in the car park behind the bar.

"Yes, no problem, we can see it from the kitchen and call you if the kitten goes inside."

We brought it down the next evening, and set the bait, then went round to the bar for a drink, and to wait. An hour passed, no kitten, typical. Nick got us a second drink. As I took only my second sip, Miguel rushed in,

"The kitten, it is inside, come quickly."

I took one more gulp of wine, it was a shame to waste it, and followed Nick. The kitten was not best pleased with being caught and was throwing itself around inside the trap. Nick covered it with a blanket, and it gradually quietened down enough to be slid into the back of the car. Back home we transferred the kitten into a large cage. It still wasn't too happy with us.

"It's ok, you're safe here, you don't have to live on chips off the floor."

It glared at me. "But I like chips," it seemed to say.

It turned out to be a girl, and we named her Dolly. When she was old enough to be spayed, Filipa said,

"When I open her, there is a lot of fat inside."

I was surprised, 'Really, she still looks quite small?"

"Yes, but under the skin is a lot of fat, very unusual for a kitten."

It must have been all those chips.

Dolly grew, and grew, and grew until she resembled a triangular doorstop, the kind filled with sand which all falls to the bottom. She has always been a very greedy girl.

Two kitten sisters came to me from a local charity, they were about eight weeks old and needed to be socialised, ready for adoption. One was jet black, the other white and tabby and we named them Peggy and Patsy. Patsy was already quite friendly, but Peggy was extremely shy and nervous. I set to work hand feeding them and playing with a fishing rod toy until both girls were quite tame. They were a very bonded pair and every time I went in to see them, they were cuddled in together or grooming each other. The weeks passed and communication with the rescue charity dwindled, no one had come forward to adopt them.

We moved them into the living room to start to integrate with the rest of the cats and they were soon accepted into our little furry family. Eventually, we forgot that they were fostered and so they just stayed. We rarely refer to them by their names as they have become known as the evil twins. Whenever there is any chance of devilment, there they are. The picture of innocence, but always ready to pounce on some unsuspecting victim, or steal a toy or two. They have one extremely cute redeeming feature, every evening Peggy starts calling for her sister. It's a strange noise, not a normal miaow or screech or yell, but a plaintive call. Patsy may be asleep on the other side of the room, but as soon as Peggy starts, she gets up and goes to her. Sometimes she gets groomed and cuddled, sometimes it's more of a nip and a headlock, but she always goes. Sisters eh!

Patsy and Peggy

18

2018, Citizenship?

We sold our rental apartment in February. I had decided to scale back the rental business due to an increasing amount of red tape under the 'Alojamento Local' law for holiday rentals. Although it was good to weed out some of the less reliable owners and agencies, I was tired of keeping up with all the changes, and there were many. The websites where I advertised were also making life difficult, increasing their charges and forcing all communications to go through them, so they could charge my clients commission too. It wasn't how I wanted to run my business.

Whilst picking up some documents from our lawyer relating to the sale, a chance remark set me a new challenge. It was after the Brexit referendum and there was a good deal of uncertainty about what it would mean for British residency in Europe. We had always been fully legal, tax-paying residents, but would that be enough? Would we need visas to live and work in Portugal? As we discussed the possible ramifications, she suddenly said,

"You should take Portuguese citizenship."

"Really? Isn't it very difficult?" It had never occurred to me that it was something to consider.

"Well, there is a process to follow, you will need some documents, a police check from the UK, your birth certificate, all translated and notarised and with an apostille, and of course, there is the language element."

"What's the language element?" I queried.

"You have to prove you have a knowledge of Portuguese, either by taking a course of lessons at an approved college, who will issue a certificate on completion or by taking an exam."

"Oh."

My Portuguese was ok, but I hadn't taken any formal lessons since the night school course before we left the UK. I was lucky that I've always had an ear for languages and spoke French pretty well, and had qualified as an EFL (English as a Foreign Language) teacher in the early 90s. However, I wasn't keen on the idea of sitting an exam, so I went home to look into what was required.

A quick search on the internet showed that I would need to achieve level A2 to support my citizenship application. It is a fairly basic level, and could be achieved by attending a college course or by taking an exam. I felt I could attempt it, but my disability meant I wouldn't be able to attend sufficient classes in the college in Portimao to pass that way. The exams were held twice a year at Faro University, so I looked up their entry requirements. It appeared that you could apply to sit the exam as an individual, so for a fee of 70€ I filled in the online form and booked myself a place at the next available opportunity, in six months time.

I bought a book of examples of past papers, the A2 level textbook and workbook and spent the summer revising and perfecting my language skills in preparation for the big day.

In the meantime, I was asked to bottle feed a litter of kittens, seven of them. They were cold when they arrived, and so, so tiny, I wasn't sure I could save any of them. There were four tabbies, one black, one white and one ginger. I had to set up two boxes so I could separate the tabbies, which were all identical, in case I fed one twice and one not all. They were too small and weak to take a bottle so I had to syringe the liquid into their mouths every two hours. On the second day, I lost the ginger one, the next morning the black one slipped away, and that evening one of the tabbies. I couldn't keep losing them at this rate, so I called the rescue,

"Ok we'll come and get the others now, and take them to the Veterinary Hospital in Portimão, they're open 24 hours for emergencies."

We arranged to meet in a local supermarket car park and carefully transferred them from one car to the other. I had only had them for a few days but I was physically and emotionally exhausted, I needed a break.

I looked for somewhere nearby and found a room available at Suites Alba, near Praia da Albandeira. Sharon came with me to help with my bags and stayed for lunch and a spa treatment in the afternoon, then Pete picked her up in the evening. I spent the next two days on my own, sleeping, reading and relaxing. I felt burnt out and needed to recharge my batteries. The rescue called on my last day, there was good news. The kittens were all doing well, although it had been touch and go. They had been diagnosed with an infection that kept causing their temperature to spike but after a course of intravenous antibiotics, they were now stable. I was so relieved that it wasn't my fault and that they were on the mend now. The next piece of good news was that they had found a mum cat with only two kittens in another rescue centre, and she had accepted my four as her own. They were now getting the best food possible, and the bonus of mummy cuddles. My email pinged with some beautiful photos of them with their new mum, they would be ok now.

At the beginning of August, we heard reports that a wildfire had broken out in Monchique. Every year there are numerous fires across the whole of Portugal. They are often extinguished fairly quickly, but every few years some get dangerously out of control, and this turned out to be one of them. It burned for days and caused many people and animals to be evacuated. A charity called Alerta coordinates information from official channels, and publishes it on their Facebook page, keeping everyone up to date with the latest developments. They also collect donations of bottled water, energy drinks and snacks which are distributed to the nearest Fire Station, and passed to the firefighters who can be on duty for days on end.

The fire raged for over a week, devastating a huge area stretching from Silves to Portimão. We could see the dark skies over the Monchique mountains, and at times we could see ash falling on Carvoeiro. It's something we are aware of when temperatures soar in the summer. Although we are quite well-protected here in a more built-up area, anyone living in the countryside has to abide by strict rules regarding clearing their land in springtime.

A few weeks later an email arrived with the schedule for my Portuguese language exam. There were four parts to it, reading, writing, listening and speaking. At 10 am we would start with reading and writing, followed by listening and then a break for lunch, with the speaking element in the afternoon. The morning session was in a group, but the afternoon consisted of appointments at 15-minute intervals for pairs of students at a time. Potentially I could be there until 4 pm, depending on how many candidates there were. Physically, this was going to be tough for me. The journey there would be painful and exhausting, along with an early start and up to six hours of sitting or standing, maybe this wasn't such a good idea after all. I explored various possibilities and discussed them with Nick.

"The only thing I can think of is if I stay in Faro the night before the exam, and get a taxi to the university, then if you can take me and pick me up the next day?"

I only ever drive locally now, Lagoa is as far as I can manage, but more usually it's to one of the nearby supermarkets or down to the village, Faro was out of the question.

"Ok, I'll take you on the Friday afternoon, then I can come back and see to the animals that evening and the following morning. Then I could come and meet you at lunchtime and wait for you to finish?"

This was getting better; we were due to have a 2-hour break for lunch so I could get some rest in the car until I was called in for the speaking element.

"Have you told the university about your mobility problems?" he asked.

"No not yet, I don't want to make a fuss, but I suppose I should."

I found an email address for the admin team and sent a message explaining about my back, and that I would need to bring my cushions with me. I received a very reassuring email acknowledging my situation and offering any help that I required. There is a pretty good awareness of disabilities in Portugal and along with the elderly and pregnant women we are allowed to 'queue jump' in most places, plus I had a letter from my GP stating that I was not to be left to wait for more than 20 minutes, at any time.

Now to find a hotel. The university is on the outskirts of Faro, to the north of the city, but there were no hotels in the vicinity. I searched for availability for the Friday night before the exam and found the closest was back towards the airport, in a fairly basic hotel, but it would be fine for just the one night.

I continued with my studies, concentrating on the listening exercises as I knew that would be my weakest point. I'm used to reading Portuguese newspapers and speaking to neighbours, but I always struggle with listening unless I already know the subject of the conversation. Unexpected questions throw me and if I miss one small word at the beginning of a sentence, it can change the whole meaning and I find myself smiling and nodding when I should be shaking my head and commiserating.

The listening exercises on the CD supplied with the book of past papers were quite simple, you'd hear someone asking for stamps, or setting up a direct debit, and have to decide where this was taking place, in a multiple-choice format. I could do that, no problem.

The big day approached and I packed as if for a week away. I had to take a pencil case with pens, pencils, erasers and sharpeners as we had to hand in all other belongings to the invigilators, it was like preparing for the first day of school.

The hotel was located just off the main dual carriageway down to the airport. Nick followed the sat nav instructions and we found ourselves in an area that we had bypassed many, many times, but had no idea it existed. We had assumed it was a fairly barren place as there were only a few apartment blocks visible from the main road, but it was actually quite a bustling little town. We drove down streets full of shops and restaurants, and past rows of houses. It was quite a revelation. Hotels, however, there were none. I double-checked the address and the pin drop on google maps, it should be just along this road. We turned around and looked again. The website showed a photo of a large building, several stories high, with a central reception area and two wings of accommodation. It should be obvious. Not to us.

We were back on the main shopping street again, with feelings of déjà vu from our first trip to Carvoeiro.

"It's got to be here somewhere," said Nick, re-setting the sat nav for the third time. "Did you check it is actually open and not just being built?"

"Well, I've got confirmation of the booking, so I doubt it's just a figment of my imagination," I replied. The strain of sitting for over an hour was beginning to affect my mood.

Nick decided to ignore the sat nav instructions and turned in the general direction of the pin drop. We were now in a completely residential area, driving on a road that ended at a wire fence. Beyond the fence was open land, but at the other end we could see the back of a large building, and proudly sat on the top of the building was a large sign HOTEL. Hooray. Just one problem, how did we get to it?

We re-traced our route and figured that if we kept taking left turns from the main road, we may find our way to the entrance. We were going away from the hotel, according to the sat nav, which was imploring us to turn around, but it had fooled us once already and we were taking control now. It took several attempts but finally, we hit on the correct combination of turns. Driving along a normal street of detached houses, we noticed a patch of open land ahead, it looked as though we were approaching the dead-end from the opposite direction. We took the last left turn before the chain-link fence, which led to a small roundabout planted with a palm tree and several small bushes, and beyond that was the Hotel. It was pure luck and had taken almost an hour,

"You have reached your destination," announced the sat nav proudly.

Thanks.

The reception area was deserted, as was the bar and restaurant area opposite. Nick brought my luggage in and we waited for a member of staff to appear. It was eerily silent, with no voices or footsteps or doors closing to be heard, perhaps it wasn't officially open after all.

Nick stepped into the bar area, where a wall-mounted TV played music videos to an empty room, the first sign of life we had come across. My back was going into spasms now and I really needed to lie down and rest, the journey had taken longer than planned and we had been standing in reception for at least twenty minutes. The whole point of arriving the day before the exam was to allow me to relax and prepare as calmly as possible, so far we had failed on all counts.

Just as I was about to give up and start looking for alternative accommodation a smartly dressed woman appeared and seemed startled to see us.

"Oh, good afternoon, can I help you?"

"Yes please, I have a reservation for one night, erm, tonight," I clarified as I handed over my Residência card.

She tapped on the computer keyboard and scanned the screen, moments passed.

"Ah yes, sorry, the system is a little slow today, but I have your booking now."

Thank goodness. Nick and I exchanged a look of relief at last. The printer on the desk chattered into life and as she took my credit card details, I signed the registration document and received my room key.

"Your room is just through those double doors and first on the left, is that ok for you?"

"That's great, thank you."

I had asked for a disabled access room, so this was perfect, with no stairs to negotiate and close to reception and the restaurant.

"Would you like to book for dinner tonight?"

"Yes please."

"The restaurant is in the bar opposite, and is open until 9 pm."

"Can I book for 7.30?"

"Yes, of course, enjoy your stay."

The room was even more spartan than I expected, with wobbly, scratched furniture, and a very basic bathroom but at least I could lie down, that made it better than the Ritz to me. Nick left to get home for feeding time and I got to relax my back and have a power nap.

I was back up at 7, ready for my dinner booking. As I entered the bar it was as empty as it had been when we arrived. I had brought some last-minute revision with me, so settled my orthopaedic cushions on a suitable chair, and waited. The TV was still on the music video channel, but silent. I spent a few minutes trying to work out which song was playing from the dance moves, it turned out to be one I had never heard of.

A check on past tenses of a couple of irregular verbs and I was starting to feel hungry. I used my walking stick to stand and made my way to the bar. It was fully stocked with optics of spirits and mixers placed on the shelves below but was lacking in anyone to serve them.

A menu lay on the side, it wasn't particularly inspiring but I spotted chicken Piri-Piri, something I often ordered in restaurants if only there was someone to tell. I wandered back to my seat; it was now 7.25.

At exactly 7.30 a smartly dressed young man strode in, he greeted me as he passed by, with a cheery "Boa noite." (Good evening)

"Boa noite," I replied. I was either the first or perhaps only booking this evening.

I followed him up to the bar and ordered a gin and tonic. He grinned and started collecting a glass, ice, lemon, then turned and gazed at the bottles lined up in front of him. He scanned them left to right and back again. I could see a bottle of Gordon's, second from the left, but he was still checking them all from side to side. On the third attempt, he let out a small sigh of triumph. There it was, hiding in plain sight, naughty Gordon.

He wasn't quite Tom Cruise but he opened the tonic with a flourish and added a slice of cucumber, presenting the glass to me with due reverence. I gave my room number, although as I appeared to be the only guest it was probably obvious.

"E para comer?" (What would you like to eat?) He enquired.

"Frango piri-piri se faz favor?" (Chicken Piri-Piri, please)

"Muito bem." (Very well)

He disappeared through a door marked 'Privado' and I returned to my seat. The food arrived surprisingly quickly, and with none of the normal kitchen noise audible from behind the 'Private' door, it seemed as if he was the barman, waiter and chef all rolled into one. The chicken was a bit dry but better than nothing, and with no companion to chat to, I was finished by 8.15. Oh well, an early night was best, given the long day ahead, so I decided to take a half bottle of wine back to my room to aid my revision.

There was a small, glass-fronted wine fridge to one side but I could only see full bottles on display.

"Desculpe senhor, tem uma pequena garrafa de vinho branco?" (Excuse me, do you have a small bottle of white wine?)

"Tenho, sim," (Yes, I have) Another bright smile, and he picked up a set of keys and tried them in the fridge lock, one by one.

The hotel guests seemed not to be big gin drinkers, or wine, it appeared. Or maybe it was just his first day. On the sixth or seventh attempt the door swung open and he crouched down to inspect the contents, bringing bottles to the front or pushing them backwards like a game of chess. No small bottles on the top shelf. The bottom shelf was almost level with the carpet, so he lay down on the floor and continued his search. I was really sorry I had asked now and hovered behind him, debating on whether to just make a run (or hobble) for it. I wasn't that desperate for a glass of wine, was I?

The search continued until a small bottle was produced from

the furthest depths of the fridge. Sustaining only a small bump to the back of the head, he stood up, straightened his shirt, smoothed his hair, and presented me with half a bottle of Monte Velho.

"Obrigadinha." (Thank you) I gave it the full 'eeenya' emphasis to show my appreciation for his efforts, quickly grabbed my cushions, textbook and stick and made my exit.

The next morning, I assumed breakfast would be served in the same place as dinner, but there was a sign on the door.

'Pequeno-almoço' ⬅ (Breakfast) I followed the arrow back through the double doors and saw another door with another sign: 'Pequeno-almoço ✓'

I opened the door and saw a long staircase going down to my left, it was so long that I couldn't see the bottom of it. There was no way I would manage that with my stick and my cushions, so much for my 'accessible' room, it just didn't come with an 'accessible' breakfast. I popped into reception to ask about room service, but only got a sad shoulder shrug and shake of the head in reply. It was lucky I'd brought a supply of emergency biscuits. While I was there, I decided to order a taxi to the university. This request was much more cheerfully received.

"A que horas?" (at what time?)

"Nove e meia por favor." (Nine-thirty, please)

The exam started at 10 and I had calculated that the journey should only take about 10 minutes. Now for the fun part.

"I need... preciso... um carro... mais alta," (I need a car higher than this)

I raised an arm above my head, with the palm of my hand

towards the ceiling and pushed it up and down. It was just as well this wasn't going to be marked as part of the exam. She looked at me, puzzled. I turned and gestured to my back.

"Não consigo dobrar, tudo metal," (I can't bend, all metal) and gave a slight bob forward.

It's so difficult to show someone that you can't do something, without doing it. I mimed getting into a car, keeping my back straight and using my hand as the car roof again. She nodded uncertainly and picked up the phone.

I gathered together everything I'd need for the exam and packed my case. We'd pick it up at lunchtime after the morning session.

My taxi arrived, a minibus just for me. The driver helped manoeuvre me into the nearest seat to the side door, it meant I didn't really have anything to hold on to, to brace myself, but we weren't going far so I hoped for the best and we were soon turning into the university car park. There were lots of people milling around, all ages from late teens to mid-sixties. I noticed a group gathered around a notice board and went to make sure I was on the list. I was amazed at just how many people were taking the exam. We were divided into five different rooms. I was in the nearest one, the amphitheatre.

A woman came out holding a clipboard and instructed us to gather by our respective rooms. We would then be called in by name and shown to our seats. All instructions were given in Portuguese so this was almost an additional part of the exam, just understanding the directions and rules. My group drifted towards the entrance hall and waited. Not just a mix of ages but also of nationalities, not as many British as I had expected but plenty of German, Dutch, Spanish, East European and Russian.

Some were individuals, like me, but others had obviously been part of college classes and gathered together, speaking in their native languages.

The door opened and two women appeared, again with clipboards, and started calling out names. One by one we started moving closer to the entrance. Just inside there was a table for all the coats and bags to be left, then clutching the few items allowed, the other candidates spread out around the large room. It was very strict, only one person every three seats along, and an empty row in front and behind. The seats were the tip-up type like in a cinema or theatre, I looked around with a sense of dread. I wouldn't be able to sit in one of these, I was sure.

I loitered by the bag and coat table until I could catch someone's eye. One of the invigilators noticed and asked what was wrong. I held up my cushions and reminded her that I had emailed regarding my disability. She checked her clipboard and nodded, gesturing for me to wait. She turned and spoke quietly to her colleague, who quickly left the room. Earlier, I had noticed a cafe just opposite the entrance to the amphitheatre, and I now watched as two men carried a table out of the cafe, through the throng of students and into the room. They set it down next to the bag and coat table and slotted a normal chair in behind. The woman I had spoken to touched my elbow and pointed towards the table. I was so grateful as I arranged my cushions and my pencil case, they couldn't have been more accommodating.

I now had a grandstand view of the rows of seats leading down to a central stage. Those who were already seated shuffled nervously, fiddling with pens and sharpening pencils. New arrivals found their seats and looked around, waving to friends and giving the thumbs up. Eventually, the doors closed and the exam could begin. The acoustics were not great and I struggled to hear what was being said on stage, but papers were being delivered to each candidate and at just after 10.05 we were instructed to turn them over and begin.

As I had hoped, the reading and writing elements were fairly straightforward. I was particularly pleased to see that we had to write a short recipe with a guide of 40 words. I decided on an omelette and thought I'd show off my vocabulary including a wide range of vegetables as well as eggs, cheese, ham and vegetable oil. The next part was to complain about a hotel room in 80 words, again, fairly easy for me after years of dealing with rental properties. I described 'ugly' furniture, 'dirty' towels and 'broken' appliances. I was just finishing listing my disappointments when I overheard another candidate's question to an invigilator. She seemed to be asking about the word counts, the invigilator shook her head and wagged a finger.

I held my hand up and asked if the number of words was a limit or a guide. A limit, don't exceed it. I checked the clock. Ten minutes to go. I checked my writing, 10 words over on the omelette. Disaster. I had to quickly remove most of the ingredients that I had added so proudly, and hope that the recipe still made sense. The hotel complaint was two words under. Phew. A bell sounded, time up. The papers were collected up and replaced with an answer sheet, this was my weakest element, the listening exercise.

After a few minutes to compose ourselves, the tape started playing. I was horrified, it was completely different from the practice papers and I was completely thrown. Instead of short sentences, it was a long story involving a dog, a suitcase, a lift, an airport, a flight... it went on and on. I looked at the answer sheet. It was multiple choice but all the answers to each question included one of the items, so question one had four options including 'dog', number two was all about 'lifts'.

We listened again and it became slightly clearer, but there were still several questions that I had to just stab at. It didn't help that the cafe was now getting ready for lunch service and as I was closest to it, I could hear their preparations louder than the tape. As the torture came to an end, I realised that several candidates were sitting with their arms folded having failed to attempt a single question. As soon as the doors opened to signify the end of the morning session, the invigilators were inundated with complaints about the complexity of the test. So, it wasn't just me that found it difficult, that was comforting at least.

Back in the reception area, I consulted the lists for the afternoon session. I had been paired with another student, his name sounded Spanish, and we would be tested on our spoken Portuguese at 2.20.

I stepped outside into the October sunshine and spotted Nick standing by the car. It seemed like years since I'd seen him, not barely 24 hours, and it was such a relief to get into the front seat, familiar and adjusted to be as comfortable as possible. I filled him in on my adventures whilst we drove back to the hotel for my luggage, then carried on down to the airport and on to the bridge to Faro Island. It was great to get away from the tension of the exam, and have lunch overlooking the sea. We arrived back just after 2 pm, the car park was much quieter now. I knew some candidates didn't need to be back until much later, but it was also highly likely that those who felt the morning hadn't gone well, had just abandoned the whole exam and gone home.

With a few minutes to go, I waited outside the designated classroom, in a corridor of identical doors. The afternoon session had started at 2 pm so the first lucky students were now leaving their room, the exam finished, for better or worse. There was a constant stream of arrivals and departures and as each new person arrived, I watched to see if they were coming to join me. A young, dark-haired guy approached, checking the number on each door, slowing down as he got closer. With a nervous smile, he sat on the other side of the door. This must be my partner. The door opened and we were called in and shown to a table in front of two invigilators. A bearded middle-aged man was behind a computer, ready to record our interaction, whilst a woman I guessed to be in her 30s, tidied a pile of laminated sheets.

After checking our identities and that we were comfortable and ready to begin, she nodded her head and the computer operator pressed a series of buttons on the keyboard. The first part of the exam was to introduce ourselves. My partner went first and I learned that he was Spanish, 28 years old, living in Faro and working at the airport. He needed to pass the exam to progress at work, and he was married with a baby daughter. I then gave a brief outline of my situation and that I was taking the exam for citizenship purposes.

Next, we had to plan a picnic together. I found it quite difficult to understand some of his pronunciation, and he may well have had the same problem with mine, but we discussed where to go, who we would invite, and what food and drink we would bring. The female invigilator asked what traditional British picnic food I would recommend, I'm not sure my description of pork pies and scotch eggs was totally understood by any of them. Sandwiches, however, were a safer bet.

Now we were almost at the end, she showed us one of the laminated pages with a list of about ten subjects. She asked us to choose one and talk about it for about three minutes. My partner chose his daughter's birth as 'The Best Day of My Life', and I chose to talk about my spinal surgery as being 'A Day I'll Never Forget'. An opportunity to use all the hospital vocabulary that I had learned during my ten days there. The computer operator clicked a few more keys and the microphone was turned off. The recordings and all our work from the morning session would now be sent up to Lisbon for marking and we could expect to receive an email with our results in 6-8 weeks.

I couldn't believe it was over, I had managed it, physically and linguistically. I had no idea whether I had passed or not, but there was nothing else I could do now but wait.

19

Camões II

The weeks passed, the weather cooled and I waited anxiously for an email. It didn't really matter if I failed, I could take the exam again next spring, but I would be very disappointed in myself if I didn't achieve even 55%. Suddenly it was December; surely I'd hear something before Christmas? The lights went up around the square and restaurants started to take bookings for the festive season, still no email. I assumed the university would close soon and resigned myself to waiting until they re-opened in January. I was so convinced that I nearly missed it when, on 20 December, an email arrived from 'Local de Aplicação de Exames'. It wasn't the normal university email address that I had used before and I almost rejected it as spam. Then one word caught my eye and I read it more thoroughly.

'Pode levantar o certificado na secretaria da Escola.'

A certificate, I could collect a certificate! The email quoted a phone number for any enquiries, so I called expecting to get a recorded message. I found myself speaking to a receptionist who put me through to the department secretary. She confirmed that I had indeed passed with 73% which was 'Bom' (Good), the middle of three grades. I couldn't believe it. Even more unbelievable was the fact that they were open until Friday 22 December. Nick made a special trip to Faro and returned with the precious certificate. The last document I needed to be able to apply for Portuguese Citizenship.

After Christmas, I made an appointment at the Conservatório in Lagoa, where they checked the paperwork and verified my signature, then along with a bank draft for 250€ I posted it all off to Lisbon. They don't send out acknowledgements, so you just have to wait and hope that the application has been received. I knew it would take a while and forgot about it for the next six months or so, but every now and then I wondered when I would hear from them.

In 2019 our magnificent Harry ze Floof was hit by a car and had to be put to sleep. Although he was getting older and slower, he was another cat who had to be allowed his freedom and would never accept being a house cat. We were lucky that it happened close to home, and Nick was able to get him to the clinic quickly, but there was nothing we or Filipa could do. Such a gorgeous boy, such a huge personality, such a huge loss.

Filipa told me about a kitten that her niece had rescued. He had suffered a severe infection in one eye, which had caused permanent damage, but he was still a cheeky little boy. She mentioned him in conversation several times, but I didn't feel ready for a new arrival, just yet.

A few weeks passed, and he was still in the clinic. He was healthy now and ready to go to a new home. I said I'd let her know if I heard of anyone suitable. Another week passed, and my phone pinged with a WhatsApp message, it was a video of Filipa and her veterinary nurse Inés. They opened a box and out jumped Camões II while they sang, a present for you, a present for you.

I gave in and Nick went to pick him up. He was the cutest, cheekiest kitten, full of mischief and fun. He loved everyone, even the grumpier cats and forced them to cuddle him, but his favourite was Rupert. At every opportunity, he would lie curled up against Rupert's tummy, or his back, or his head, and they would sleep like that for hours. Rupert has always had a dedicated group of feline followers, but none that he allowed as close, and as often, as Camões. They had a very special relationship.

Lucy, beautiful little Lucy, our oldest cat and the one who started us off on our cat rescue journey, finally left us for the last time. She was a one-off, a constant presence, and we feel her absence every day. Her enduring legacy is all the little lives we have saved since, because of her. Because of that first day that she walked into our rental villa and past our dogs at the time, Gem and Samson. She gave us the courage to take in Ginger and Camões, knowing the dogs had accepted her first. What a character, we'll always remember her.

I took Nancy from a rescue centre, for socialising. Guess what? She stayed. She is so cute, black and white, with huge green eyes. She seemed to stop growing at about six months old and between her and Dolly, I think we must have both the fattest, and the smallest cats in the Algarve.

After my trip to Suites Alba, I was keen to investigate other similar hotels nearby. I have quite a checklist. There has to be a walk-in shower, a lift, and room service. The spa has to provide a range of treatments, not just massages, as I still can't bear anyone to touch my back. I like facials, head massage, reflexology, reiki, pedicures and foot and leg massage. More top and toe than top-to-toe. It was surprisingly difficult to find one place that ticked all the boxes, but then I found the Monchique Resort and Spa.

I booked a 3-night stay and mentioned it to Sharon, who was

keen to come too. She could drive us there in my car, and be my carer and cushion carrier. We packed the car with enough clothes and snacks for a fortnight and left Nick and Pete in charge.

It only takes about twenty to thirty minutes to get to the hotel, so we set off in time for lunch, and then check-in at 3 pm. We sat outside on the restaurant balcony, overlooking the swimming pool and enjoyed salads and cocktails. The view was spectacular and so different from being on the coast, although due to the altitude (we were almost at the highest point in the Algarve), we could still see the ocean in the distance. After lunch, we went to check in and pick up our room keys.

I had explained about my mobility problems when making the reservation, and they had allocated us adjoining rooms, just a short walk from the restaurant. A member of staff accompanied us to our rooms, wheeling our luggage on a trolley. When he opened the door to my room, I was surprised at how spacious it was. There was a separate living room/kitchen with a fridge, hob, microwave and dishwasher, and a bedroom with an en-suite bathroom. I went to check on the shower situation and was horrified to see a bath with a shower over. This wasn't what I had booked. He was now showing Sharon into her room next door, so I went to ask about my walk-in shower.

"Yes madam, you have a walk-in shower," he confirmed.

"No, I don't, I have a bath with a shower, I can't step into a bath."

"Excuse me," he turned to Sharon, "I'll be back in a moment. Please follow me."

We returned to my room and went inside. He turned and

closed the front door, then opened another door which had been hidden behind it. Inside was another bathroom, with a walk-in shower.

"So, I have two bathrooms?"

"Yes madam, every room has two bathrooms."

"Oh, I didn't realise, thank you." I passed him a five euro note to cover my embarrassment.

The rest of our stay was great, we relaxed at the spa, ate and drank our way through both the restaurant menu and the supplies we had brought with us, and soon we were heading back down towards home. It's probably as far as I'll travel now, but we decided we would be back soon.

Two kittens appeared in one of our neighbour's gardens, while Nick and I were taking Rupert and Henry on our regular evening dog walk. They looked to be around three to four months old. One was black and very feral; the other was ginger and white and slightly friendlier. The house was a holiday rental so it was unlikely there would be anyone staying there until spring so they seemed to have made the garden their home. Every night they waited in the same place for us to turn up and leave their food.

We had just got used to Camões and his antics when he suddenly became listless and reluctant to eat. We went through the usual blood tests and scans and received the devastating news that he had also developed lymphoma. Memories of Monty flooded back. They were similar in lots of ways, both cheeky and cuddly, mischievous and affectionate. I decided I wasn't going to put Camões through the same ordeal that Monty had suffered. We took the treatment offered and gave him what time we could, but as soon as we could see his condition was deteriorating, we said our goodbyes. He was with us less than a year, but it seemed a lot more. He had so much to give and he really lived every day, as though he knew his time was limited. He was a very special boy.

At the same time, Elsie fell ill and was in and out of hospital. Nick managed to see her on his last UK trip in March, just before the Covid pandemic took hold. We felt there was something seriously wrong, but no one seemed to know exactly what it was.

20

Lulu, Ella and Co

In the end, it was about 18 months before I received a letter, with a Portuguese birth certificate attached, and instructions to make an appointment to apply for my Cartão de Cidadão. It was now May 2020, in the first few months of the Covid pandemic and appointments were hard to come by. I checked availability for several places and found the quickest was in Portimão, in 2 weeks.

I was nervous as I queued outside, waiting my turn, but it was fairly straightforward. I handed over my new birth certificate and my old Cartão de Residência, signed a form, had my height and fingerprints taken, and finally a photograph. My new card would be sent to the Lagoa office and I would be notified when it was ready for collection. Ten days later I emerged clutching my card, a fully legal Portuguese citizen, at last.

We were still feeding the two kittens every evening. The ginger and white kitten became much friendlier and would allow me to stroke her while she ate. Her fur was thin and sparse, and usually full of grass seeds, but she let me remove them without showing any aggression. She seemed to enjoy the attention but was never happy to be picked up or carried. We named her Lulu. The black one would hiss at us and stay well out of touching distance behind a thick hedge, and only began to eat after we had walked away. We named her Ella.

Lulu

"We'll have to try and catch these two before they get pregnant. I'll try to get Lulu tame enough to pick up, to make it less stressful for her."

We were now in lockdown so the house remained empty. Every evening I placed her food on the garden wall and stood and talked to her, while she headbutted my hand. It felt very strange to be at the start of the main season, but with everywhere being so quiet. I smoothed out her fur and removed dead leaves and even some pretty little blue petals. She would still get jumpy if I tried to pick her up but we were making good progress.

A few nights later, she came running to us as usual, but as I started to slide the food out of the pouch, I suddenly became aware of a movement behind the fence. Three tiny kittens had followed her but had stayed behind the chain link, out of reach. There hadn't been any sign that she was pregnant and I felt so sorry for her, having gone through her pregnancy on our one meal a day, plus whatever she could catch. Then giving birth in the wild and raising and protecting these little scraps. They looked healthy as far as I could see, she had obviously done a great job but now we had 5 to feed, and 3 kittens to catch and re-home.

There was one pretty calico, which was the smallest, a cute ginger and white, like his mum, and the largest and feistiest was a pure ginger. They didn't appear every day, and when we didn't see them, we worried about them, had something happened to them? A dog? A car? An illness? Then the next night their little heads would pop up and we would heave a sigh of relief. We started taking an empty cat carrier with us each time, hoping that we would find a way to reach them.

About a week after we had first seen them, the smallest calico kitten managed to wriggle through the fence, desperate to get to the food that her two siblings were devouring. She had decided to come directly to the source as the bigger kittens tried to elbow her out of the way. As she reached our side of the fence, she briefly turned her back to me. I took a chance and managed to grab her, and before she knew it, she was safe inside the cat box.

We hurried home with one tiny, petrified kitten, around 4

weeks old, and named her Cilla, as she was a surprise. Although she was terrified, she wasn't at all aggressive and with a bit of love and attention she was soon eating from my hand and allowing me to pick her up. I put the word out on social media, hoping to find a good home for her as she was fast becoming a little sweetheart. I quickly received a message from someone I knew from other animal rescue organisations and situations, and I was more than happy for her to make her new home with them and the rest of their cat family.

Meanwhile, we continued feeding Ella and Lulu and tried to catch the remaining two kittens. Having seen their sister disappear into a box, never to be seen again, they were more cautious. They were also getting bigger so it was more difficult for them to squeeze through the fence, and they stayed uncaptured, behind the wire mesh. Over the next few days, we concentrated on trying to gain their trust. We brought tempting titbits of roast chicken or tuna, letting them see we were providers of the good stuff and worth getting to know.

One part of the fence was a little loose, so we started leaving the food near this small gap, and one evening the ginger and white kitten poked his head and shoulders through, finding the aroma of tinned sardines irresistible. I had to make a snap decision, if you try to catch a cat or kitten and fail, then it's game over and you might as well call it a day and go home. You only get one chance and if you blow it they won't come near you again until the next day, at least. I held my nerve, stood completely still and barely took a breath while he was distracted by the food and happily munched away. I closed my hand around his tiny, warm body and popped him straight into the cat box. Kitten 2, named Mango by my young cousin, Freya, was safely caught and transferred to a cage in our hospital/nursery wing.

Again, he proved to be very friendly after a short period of adjustment, but he was lonely, having been used to spending all his time with his mum, brother and sister. He would cry for me to pick him up, and purr loudly while enjoying cuddles. This made me all the more determined to get the last kitten and to catch and spay the adults to stop them from having any more litters of unwanted kittens. It's a huge problem here in the Algarve, kittens can become pregnant at 5 or 6 months, and produce two litters per year. If only 6 kittens survive each year, and none are neutered, within 4 years that one female can have more than 2000 descendants, so it can quickly get out of control.

We went back every night, armed with our trusty cat box. Kitten 3 had always been the biggest and most feral, and after a few near misses he disappeared for a few nights and we thought we had lost any chance of catching him. Once they get to around 8 weeks old, it becomes more and more difficult to just pick them up without risking severe injury from their small but razor-sharp teeth and claws.

He reappeared 3 or 4 days later, obviously very hungry. Maybe he had managed to get shut in somewhere, but he was desperate for food, so he came to us and we got him into the box without too much fuss. I couldn't believe we had managed to get all 3 of them to safety.

We kept the boys in separate cages for the first 24 hours, just in case they didn't recognise each other. However, it soon became clear that not only did they know they were brothers, but they wanted to be reunited, so we put them together and they became inseparable. They played, cuddled, and slept together, it was so lovely to see them, they were definitely a bonded pair. Mango was still very happy to be picked up for a cuddle, but Lenny, also named by my cousin, (thank you again Freya) stayed towards the back of the cage and was reluctant to get too close to us. If he was in the right mood, or we had some tasty titbits he would allow us to stroke him, but we didn't attempt to pick him up.

Again, I advertised them on social media with cute photos, but sadly there were no serious responses. I emailed photos to our vet, Filipa, who put up a poster in the clinic reception area, in case any of her clients were looking for a new kitten, or two, but still no response. We were just about to resign ourselves to keep them until they were big enough to be neutered, then setting them free. This process is referred to as TNR (Trap, Neuter, Release) and is normally used for adults who can't be tamed, when an email pinged into my inbox, the clinic had someone interested… in Mango. My heart sank, Mango was the cutest and friendliest, and I didn't want to deny him the chance of a lovely home, but he was so close to Lenny. I couldn't decide what to do for the best. I decided to be a bit cheeky and ask if the potential new owner would take them both.

I think it is always a good idea to get two kittens rather than one, as they can be very playful and get bored easily on their own. It also saves your hands and feet from being cut to ribbons, if they have another kitten to play fight with. Thankfully, they quickly agreed, and I was so relieved, it was the best possible solution. It was only then that I found out that the person who wanted to take them was an employee at the clinic that I knew well. They had a small-holding out in the country which would be a perfect home for the boys so I happily handed them over, knowing I had done the best for them. Now to TNR Lulu and Ella.

Lulu still waited for us in the same place every evening and started calling out to us as we approached. Ella gladly ate our food, but glared at us and hissed if we came too close. We were going to have to bring in the big guns to have any chance of catching her. Fortunately, Cliff offered to loan us his cat trap again, but we couldn't leave it unattended as a) it wasn't ours, b) we'd have to try to trap her in a public place and c) we couldn't leave a cat in a trap for several hours in temperatures of 30+ degrees in the height of summer.

Nevertheless, we took the trap down one evening, and helped by a neighbour, manoeuvred it into a suitable place, baited it with some tasty food and waited, and waited. Both cats appeared immediately, smelt the food, and circled the trap, clearly suspicious of this new contraption and wondering why their dinner was behind bars.

Again, we stood stock still, not even a whisper passed between us, as we tried to watch proceedings, but also stay out of sight of the cats. We waited a bit longer, willing one of them to take the bait. There were a few false starts when they put one foot in the trap, but didn't go far enough to trigger the door to snap shut. It was starting to get dark, and we hadn't eaten yet ourselves so we decided to call it a day, but just as we were going to remove the trap, Ella took one step, then another, unable to resist the lure of the food any longer. As she approached the dish, she stepped on the pressure pad which released the door and suddenly the trap sprang shut.

Ella went berserk, throwing herself against the sides of the trap. We knew this was likely to happen so had brought a large blanket to throw over the cage to help her calm down. It also helped to save our hands from her fury, as we now had to pick it up with an extremely irate cat inside. The trap is made of a sturdy metal mesh and there were plenty of opportunities for her to draw blood.

Back home we transferred her to the cage recently vacated by Mango and Lenny. She was still furious and sat glaring at us through the bars. We added a litter tray, more food and some water while she retreated to one corner, scowling, not taking her eyes off us. We had to keep her for a few days until Filipa could operate on her, so we risked bodily harm every time we opened the cage to change her litter tray or replace her food.

When the day came to take her up to the clinic, we had to decide how to transport her. The cage she was in was too big to move, so we had left the trap inside, and had to persuade her to get back into it. No easy feat. First of all, we had to prime and bait it from outside the large cage, with limited access and a large, angry cat watching our every move. This time she was wiser and showed zero interest in the sardines we placed inside. We'd tried the easy way, so we had to put a bit more effort in. Using the plastic rods from a fishing rod cat toy, we took up positions at either end of the cage and 'persuaded' her down to the entrance of the trap. We didn't expect that she would jump straight over it and that the resulting thud would activate the door. An hour of effort resulted in us trapping a dish of sardines.

We started again, this time blocking her escape routes as we went until finally, she had no choice but to step into the trap. A slight nudge and her rear paws were inside, and we triggered the trap manually. Success! We were able to transport her to the clinic and the following day she was spayed and we had saved innumerable numbers of unwanted kittens from being born.

After 24 hours under observation, we brought her home for 10 days of recuperation, for her stitches to heal and for a course of antibiotics, and so our battle of wits continued. Her absence hadn't made her heart any fonder, and, unsurprisingly, we were still very much the enemy, even though we put the aircon on for her, and gave her a fleecy blanket to cuddle into. We all survived the next 10 days, just about, and finally, she was allowed her freedom. We had to coax her back into the trap, but we had learnt from the last time, and it went much more smoothly. We got her into the car and drove down to the end of the cul-de-sac where we had caught her, a whole two weeks earlier. We stopped the car, opened the trap, and with the tiniest hesitation, she leapt out and ran off down the road. There was no way we would ever have managed to tame her; this was where she was happiest and we had to respect that. Of course, we would still come and feed her every evening. One ear had been clipped, to signify to anyone who found her that she had already been spayed, so we knew we would always recognise her.

Now for Lulu. Although she was now almost tame, she was still not prepared to let me pick her up. One night I tried to gently lift her front paws and she sank her teeth into my hand, and then applied a little more pressure, just to make sure I'd got the message. She ran off with her tail high, swishing from side to side and I walked home with blood running down my arms.

As Covid travel restrictions began to lift, most of the rental villas around us were now filling up with holidaymakers, many of them had driven from Spain and Northern Portugal and brought their dogs with them. This unnerved Lulu, and we didn't see her every night, so we left her food in the usual place and hoped she'd come for it. I was so glad we had caught the kittens to save them from being chased, or worse. We gave up trying to catch her under these circumstances until September came, the schools reopened, and our road started to quieten down again.

Nick left on a week-long work trip, and for some unknown reason, I decided to try to catch Lulu on my own. I don't know what I was thinking. However, one evening I loaded the car with a small metal cage, food and blankets and drove the short distance to Lulu's hangout. She was waiting in what had become her normal place, on a wall about waist height. I placed the cage on the wall, but unfortunately, the cage was wider than the wall so I had to lean against it to keep it in place. Lulu approached, and although she smelt the food, she waited and watched for several minutes. I stroked her, and talked to her, trying to edge her close to the cage, but every time she got nearer, she pulled away, two steps forward and three back.

I dropped some tuna at the entrance to the cage. That got her attention. She took a step forward just as a car drove past, and she retreated once again. I'm not the most patient of people and my back and hips were aching from leaning against the cage for so long. I took some more of the tuna and smeared it on her face and mouth, she licked some of the oily mush and decided she'd like a bit more. She took a step, stretched her neck out and grabbed the piece I'd dropped at the entrance. I quickly dropped another piece further in, again she took a step and snatched at it, her front two paws were now inside. I hardly dared breathe, as she took another step towards the dish of food. This was crucial, if anything went wrong now, I'd have wasted the whole evening, and there would be no chance of catching her tonight.

She hesitated for the longest time. Sniffing the air, desperate for the tuna but looking around and weighing up her options. Suddenly the temptation was too much and with another step, she had 3 feet inside the cage. I had to take this chance, and quickly. I tapped her rear end, urging her forward, and reached for the door, closing it quickly but gently, and locking it securely behind her.

She looked round in mild surprise but didn't thrash around as Ella had, but calmly carried on eating. I couldn't believe it. I had managed it on my own, I was elated.

Then the reality hit, it was getting dark and I had to move a heavy cage and an adult cat into the car. It was only a few feet away but my disability meant that I couldn't manhandle it easily. Thankfully I had thought to put my keys in my pocket, and pressed the remote to unlock the doors, then balancing the cage on one leg I slid the door open and nudged the cage onto the back seat.

A short drive home and I had the opposite problem, how to get the cage and Lulu into our hospital wing. Although not far, I had to pass through two gates, and up a couple of steps, I hadn't actually thought of the practicalities in my rush to catch her. A sudden flash of inspiration, I had a tartan shopping trolley which I used to store the recycling before taking it to the respective bins, so I brought it out and managed to balance the cage on top. It wasn't particularly steady, as the trolley was smaller than the cage, and it had a soft fabric top so I had to keep one hand on it while opening and closing the gates, and then struggled to lift it up the steps, but finally, it was on the table, safe and secure.

The large cage was still there, waiting for her, and it was easy to transfer her into it. She settled in fine, such a difference from Ella. She was so used to me that she positively enjoyed the extra cuddles now she was with me 24/7. I made an appointment for her to be spayed, but it would be a few days before they could fit her in, that was fine as she was so easy to look after. I popped in every few hours to keep an eye on her.

Around 4 p.m. I made one such visit, just to clean her litter tray and check her water and biscuits, but as I opened the door she looked to be in pain. Her whole body was rigid, and she was making a strange mewling sound. As I watched, she relaxed, and then tensed again, a wave passing down her back, it looked as though she were having contractions. She shifted slightly and to my amazement, there was a small blob lying beside her. She gave it a sniff but it was obvious to both of us that although she had given birth, it wasn't a viable kitten. I had to reach in and remove it. Once again there had been no indication that she had been pregnant - and so soon after her previous litter.

She was calmer now and I was just about to leave when she started to tense up again, and another little blob appeared. I waited a little longer, I had no idea how many times it was going to happen. Ten minutes later a third blob appeared and Lulu seemed to know immediately that it was all over and started to clean herself up. I changed all her bedding and cleaned the cage. By the time I had disposed of everything and went back to see her, she was back to normal. Clean and calm and you'd never have known what had just happened. Animals are amazing creatures.

A few days later and she was spayed, the vet could tell she had been carrying 3 embryos but luckily there was no infection and her operation and recovery were otherwise uneventful. As with Ella, we had to keep her for 10 days recovery time, but unlike Ella, she was becoming tamer and tamer and I was beginning to dread having to let her go. The problem was that we already had too many cats plus 2 dogs, and we had never introduced an adult cat into our furry family, only very young kittens. Some of the cats were still quite feral and I wasn't sure that it would work. As the time to release her got closer, we decided to take a chance on moving her cage into the house, just to see what the reaction would be.

A few of the cats approached the cage and gave her a suspicious sniff. Lulu just sat there, there was no hissing or spitting, it was all strangely calm. One, in particular, Doris, who I had bottle fed since she was one day old, was very interested and spent most of her time lying next to, or even on top of the cage. I wasn't sure if she was being friendly or whether she was acting as a jailor or guard.

After a few days, we opened the cage door and waited to see if they would all remain as calm. Doris was there as usual and immediately stepped inside the cage, inspecting the litter tray, and then the food bowl to see if Lulu had something better. Once again, Lulu didn't react, she just sat and watched, not at all territorial. As Doris left, Lulu followed and started to investigate the living room, there were still no reactions, no growling or fights. I was completely astounded.

Every day Lulu became a bit braver and explored further, but we put her back in the cage each night, just in case anything kicked off while we were asleep. After a week or so we were confident that she had been accepted as one of the tribe, so removed the cage, and she found her own little space to sleep. She also had access to the 'catio' and that's where she spends her days now, showing no sign of trying to escape. She has never tried to slip out of the door when we come in and out, and there have never been any problems between her and the other cats. In the evenings she comes in and drapes herself over me, getting as close to me as she possibly can, my little shadow. She's one amazing cat.

The news from Berkshire wasn't good. Elsie wasn't coping at home, even with carers, and she moved into a local care home. Sadly, she was only there for a few weeks when she died peacefully, just days after her 90th birthday.

The funeral was arranged for the end of August, but due to the travel restrictions in place, it seemed unlikely that Nick would be able to attend. Nevertheless, we wrote our tribute to be included in the eulogy, along with Nick's brothers' recollections. Elsie's love of her time spent in Carvoeiro got several mentions from all three of them. The funeral director organised for the service to be broadcast online, and we planned to watch it from here, just me, Nick and mum.

To our astonishment, a week before the funeral, it was announced that Portugal was to be added to the green list of countries who could travel to the U.K. Nick quickly booked flights and a hotel, he would only stay two nights and would quarantine as much as possible, but he was able to attend after all. Mum and I still watched the service online together.

21

2021, On the road with Nick

With a combination of Brexit and now Covid, Nick has stopped work trips to the UK, probably for good. He enjoyed most of them, but some do still stick in his memory. In the early days, when quarantine was still six months, a cat he was carrying was refused travel. He had no choice but to leave it at the vet, and pick it up again on his way back. The vet who had messed up the paperwork looked after it until it was able to travel again.

There was the time he agreed to take a woman, her dog, and her belongings to England, then found out she was travel-sick and they had to drive through the snow in northern Spain with the window open.

Several times the pet passports have been wrong and he has had to make a mad dash to a Spanish or French vet to make the necessary corrections.

Once, he arrived at Dieppe to be told that he had to wait another three days before the passport for the cat he was carrying was legal, so he had to kick his heels in a hotel and re-book his ferry ticket. Another woman travelling with her cat forgot to make sure the cat box was closed securely when they stopped at a service station. When they returned to the van, the box was empty and there was no sign of the cat, then they heard a noise coming from behind the panel under the dashboard. It had found a tiny space and squeezed in behind, they opened a tin of cat food and waited for two hours until it made its way back out again.

Twice he broke down and had to abandon his trips. The first time he was only in Faro, and he had to find a colleague to transport a woman and her five cats to France. On this occasion, he had a lucky escape as she let one of the cats out at a service station, and it took twelve hours to persuade it down from a tree. The second time was on a Spanish motorway. The van was towed to the nearest garage, and Nick came home by taxi, a journey of 300 kilometres.

He became an expert on pet travel rules and often advised vets on the process. He knew the Brittany Ferries summer and winter timetables by heart, and all the crews recognised him as he travelled with them so frequently.

It's the end of a long and significant part of our lives, although he will probably still do European trips if they come up.

We noticed Amber seemed to be having trouble eating and she had started to ignore her breakfast and dinner. We tried giving her soft pate, and sachets of wet food in gravy, but she just licked at them. She was very independent and reluctant to be caught, but after a few attempts, we succeeded in getting her into a box and up to the clinic. Filipa was pleased to see her again until she examined her mouth.

"I'm afraid she has a big problem with the teeth and gums. It is common with street cats, maybe a sign she has some other immunity problem. The only permanent solution is to remove the teeth."

"Oh no, we can't put her through that, is there no other treatment?"

"Well, I can give cortisone to reduce the inflammation, and we can see if it helps."

She gave Amber an injection plus some antibiotics and we brought her home. There was a huge improvement almost immediately, which lasted for about a month.

"I can give another injection, bring her to me."

So we did and kept taking her back when we saw the cortisone begin to wear off.

Walking down to feed Ella, we found a strange cat in a neighbouring garden. He was large, grey and white, and very similar to a British Shorthair. I stopped to feed him through the fence and saw that he was thin and covered in cuts and scars, probably from fighting, so it was likely that he hadn't been neutered. However, he seemed very friendly and tried to reach out to me. He was there every evening and with every meal, he got braver and came closer.

Nick and Steve went off to Armona Island, next to Farol, off the coast of Olhão, for a fishing trip. I go to a spa for a break, and he goes fishing or golfing. Once again, I made the ridiculous decision to try and catch the new cat on my own. Using the same method as for Lulu, I coaxed him into the metal cage and brought him back. He was very docile and purred as I stroked him through the bars. I texted mum, Anne-Marie and Rhona, Freya's mum, to let them know. I joked that I deserved a gin and tonic for my efforts, maybe a Sharish, a Portuguese brand that is one of my favourites. Perhaps that should be his name, a reply bounced back, Omar Sharish, so he became Omar.

I made an appointment to have him checked over, then neutered, and brought him home to recover. He was looking so much better now, he had put on weight and his wounds were healing nicely, he was turning into a really handsome boy. Again, we advertised him, and again, we had no enquiries. I felt it was best for him to be released back where we found him, and we would continue to feed him and keep an eye on him. Now he was neutered he would be less likely to get himself into trouble or wander very far.

The first night we went to look for him, he had disappeared. We checked all the nearby gardens, and found him a little further down the road, up a tree. He wasn't very high up but didn't seem to be able to find his way back down again. I used my walking stick to tap on the trunk and get his attention, then guide him down. He recognised me and came to be fed. The next night he had moved again and we found him peering over a wall, about eight feet high. We were there until it got dark, trying to work out how he had got up there, and how we could entice him down. I threw some biscuits towards him and had to call it a night.

The next day I went back and worked out that he was behind a row of townhouses. The gate was unlocked so I walked around the block until I reached the terrace behind the high wall but there was no sign of him, although it did reassure me that he wasn't trapped. That evening when we went looking for him, he was on the same terrace so Nick followed the path that I had taken in the morning, and when Omar saw him, he climbed over the edge and walked down the wall, gripping the surface with his paws.

He wasn't coping back in the outside world so we made a plan to catch him again. We thought it would be easy, he was used to us and pretty friendly, but he refused to be picked up. We went back with oven gloves, thanks for the tip Pete, and got him into a cage.

This time we thought we would try him with the indoor cats, so moved him into a cage in the living room. The other cats accepted him, quite well, but he must have been chased by dogs at some point because he was terrified of them and actually went for Rupert a couple of times. It wasn't safe for us to keep him but he wasn't safe outside either. I suspected he may have some sight problems, given his inability to jump down from the tree. I was at a loss, he was a lovely boy, but he couldn't stay.

I called Corrine at the Carvoeiro Cat Charity and asked if they would take him in their shelter if we sponsored him. She said she would take him if he was negative for feline AIDS and leukaemia, which he was, and he had already had his vaccinations, so Nick took him to join the rest of their rescues. I was really sad to say goodbye to him, but I knew he would be safe there, and who knows, maybe a volunteer might find him irresistible.

Another milestone birthday was looming, where do the years go? Nick was turning sixty. I couldn't believe it, sixty. I was stumped for ideas for a present. I couldn't organise a special trip, between my mobility issues and the pandemic. He doesn't like jewellery, and didn't need any clothes, what could I get him? He does like a glass of port, so I ordered a bottle from 1961, his birth year. I still needed something else... I know, I would commission a painting or drawing of all the dogs we had had since we had been together. I counted them up. There was Sabre, a gorgeous German Shepherd that Nick already had when I met him. Then Gem and Samson, Barney, Nikas, Maisie, Henry and Rupert. Eight. I started looking for old photos of the first three and searching my phone for the others.

I asked on Facebook for recommendations of a local artist, and several people mentioned the same person. I sent her a message to enquire about the cost and feasibility and received a detailed reply. I felt that I had found the right person. I explained that it was going to be a surprise for his birthday, so we would have to be discreet. How could we meet up? I didn't have an excuse to leave the house as Nick was used to doing all the shopping and running errands, to the chemist for example, and if I had a doctor's appointment, he drove me there and back.

If Leanne came to the house, I couldn't guarantee that he wouldn't just pop home for lunch or to pick up some tools or something he'd forgotten.

Sharon and I had booked another trip to Monchique so I suggested Leanne could meet us at the hotel for lunch during our stay, and my secret would be safe. As I chose photos that I could send to Leanne, I began to think about the cats we have had. There were so many, but maybe I could pick out eight that would represent them all, then we could have two pictures. Lucy had to be there, as our first one, little Doris being bottle fed as a nod to all the pups and kittens I had raised, definitely Harry, then Monty, Smokey, Mabel, Camões II and finally Lulu. I gave Leanne the good news, I had just doubled her workload.

We met at the hotel and spent several hours discussing the project on the restaurant terrace. We worked on the layout and I gave Leanne some more information on the animals and their stories, so she could get a feel for their personalities.

For weeks messages flew back and forth, requests for more photos from different angles, and close-ups for eye and nose colours. Leanne was meticulous in getting every detail right. A few weeks before the big day she was ready to deliver them, framed and mounted and ready to be displayed.

Nick had a busy week planned, and told me he would be out every day, until around 5 pm. This was our chance. I gave Leanne directions to the house, excited to see the outcome of weeks of planning. Ten minutes before she was due to arrive, the phone rang,

"That job this afternoon has been postponed, they're not ready for us yet, so I'll come home for lunch, then come back to sort out the warehouse later."

Of all the days.

"Erm, is it worth coming home just to go back again? Maybe you'd be better to stay and do whatever you're doing, and then come home later, and you're in for the day?"

"I could I suppose, I was just going to grab some lunch."

"No, I think it's better to carry on, you might not feel like going back out again."

"Ok, I'll get lunch here and see you about 4 o'clock."

"Ok, see you later."

As I put my phone down it buzzed again,

"I'm here."

The portraits were brilliant, I was so pleased with them, and I knew Nick would be too. It was the perfect present and we would be able to see their little faces all the time.

With all the Covid restrictions in place, we could only plan a small celebration for Nick's birthday. We invited mum, Lynne and Steve and Maria to join us at Mar d'Fora, a lovely restaurant overlooking Praia do Paraíso. I ordered a cake from a local bakery as a surprise, and Maria picked it up for me and brought it to the restaurant. I bought decorations for the cake, and also for the garden, and after he left for work in the morning, I strung banners and streamers along the front fence, just to make sure everyone passing would see them. I wasn't sure how he would react, but he was pretty good-humoured about it all.

When he opened his presents at the restaurant, he was delighted with the animal portraits, recognising all their little faces immediately.

"Where did you… how… oh Barney, Nikas, Lucy!"

He looked from one to the other, taking it all in with tears in his eyes. Leanne had hoped for a good reaction, and I think we got it.

After about six months of treatment Amber's injections were only lasting three weeks, then two. She started to run away from us, knowing that if we caught her, she would be getting an injection. It was upsetting to see her become so wary of us as she had always been so friendly. At the same time, Coco developed a runny nose, which I assumed to be some type of sinus infection, so she went up for an examination.

I managed to catch Amber asleep one afternoon and gently put her in a cat box we had left out ready. While I waited for Nick to come and get her, I tried hand feeding her a small amount of chicken, but she started to gag and paw at her mouth. This was something new, and not a good sign. Filipa checked her mouth and found that she had a tumour growing that was like a second tongue. It was starting to block her airway; this must be why she started to panic with the chicken in her mouth. There was nothing for it but to make the decision then and there. She had been doing well on the cortisone injections so we hadn't been prepared to lose her just yet.

Coco was put on anti-biotics, but Filipa decided to take her to Claudia for an x-ray, just to check whether there was an underlying problem. The news wasn't good.

"She has a tumour behind the nose, it appears to be aggressive and is already invading the eye socket. It is not in the brain… yet," she tailed off.

"But it could go there, soon?"

"It could, and anyway it will continue to grow into the eye socket."

"We can't let her continue like that."

"I know. I'm so sorry."

In just ten days we had lost two of our lovely girls. It was a heavy blow.

22

Puppy brothers

Just after I began writing this book, I received a call from Filipa.

"Good morning, how are you?" I said as I answered the phone.

"My dear, I am so tired."

"Why, what's wrong?"

"The reason is why I am calling you."

I guessed what was coming next.

"Yesterday I received a present."

"Puppies or kittens?"

"Puppies, four, in a cardboard box by the door of the clinic when I arrived."

Unfortunately, this was not a rare event. There is a reluctance amongst some Portuguese to spay and neuter their dogs and cats, believing it to be unhealthy and unnatural. There are many campaigns and discussions around neutering, but still, the unwanted puppies and kittens come, so far I have successfully hand-reared 16 pups.

"I had to call and ask, could you take two?" Filipa continued, "we can cope with two here but four is too many."

"Yes, of course, Nick was coming to see you anyway to make an appointment for Henry's annual vaccinations, I'll tell him to bring the pups home."

An hour later Nick pulled up and brought a small cat carrier into our nursery/sick room. I had prepared a small cage with blankets and a stuffed toy for them to cuddle into, and we transferred them along with one of the fleece blankets from the travel box, so they had something familiar. They were tiny, two little boys that could easily fit in the palm of my hand. One was mostly black with patches of white, the other was white with black spots, like a miniature Friesian cow. These poor little scraps had been taken from their mum at about 5 days old, their eyes still tightly closed. She would be frantically looking for them, and they, being used to her milk, were reluctant to take a bottle. It's so sad that it still happens.

No matter how many times I have bottle fed puppies and kittens it's always daunting. The first few days are particularly nerve-wracking until you, and they, settle into a routine. It's physically and emotionally draining, keeping an eye on the clock and feeding them every three to four hours. I constantly worry about them being too hot or too cold and drinking too much or too little. They also have to be 'toileted' as they are unable to wee and poo on their own. Luckily, no one can hear me as I sit with a baby in one hand and a pad of loo roll in the other, gently massaging them and saying, 'come on poo, I can see you, out you come.'

Less than a week after I started looking after them, the black puppy began to cause concern. From being a strong, wriggly puppy, he suddenly seemed weaker, unable to hold his head up. He felt lighter and less solid in my hand and was reluctant to feed. Each time I went in to see them I felt nervous, unsure of what I would find, and anxiously searched to see if both of them were still breathing. When he was still floppy the following day,

I had to make a decision.

I don't generally like to syringe-feed them as it's easy to give them too much, and they can choke or aspirate the milk into their lungs, but at this stage, I had to try. Gently cradling his head in one hand and the syringe in the other, I stroked his throat with my little finger, to encourage him to swallow the minute amount of milk. After a short rest, I introduced another few millilitres into his mouth and watched as he swallowed it down. He gradually drank ten, then fifteen ml, approximately 3 teaspoons' full. There was nothing else I could do but wait and hope.

Although his brother was smaller, he was still as vigorous as before and happily took the bottle. When their next feed was due, I was prepared for bad news, but as I opened the cage door the black puppy stumbled towards me. I caught my breath and my eyes welled up to see him. He was a fighter and it looked as though he had turned the corner. When I offered him the bottle, this time he took it, and with a little encouragement started to suck, I could feel the strength and weight returning to his tiny body. After both had been fed and toileted, I put them back into their cat carrier with fresh fleece blankets, they cuddled up together as usual and I saw his brother place one little paw around his shoulder.

At the next feed he was completely back to normal, and happily drank 20 ml of milk. He was back with us. Once again, I was reminded how fragile they are at that age, how quickly they can go down, but with care and a dash of luck they can come back up just as rapidly.

In the first few days I was making 100 ml of milk formula, and throwing some away but a few days after his recovery their intake increased to more than a bottle between them, four times a day. Where I had had to encourage them to take the bottle, they now almost grabbed it hungrily. They grew rapidly and first the black puppy, and then his brother's eyes opened, at almost three weeks old.

Now it was time to move them out of the cat carrier and into a larger cage, with space to move around as they gained in size and strength, particularly in their hind legs, which were now able to support them. It would be a few days before they could focus properly but they were now becoming toddlers instead of babies.

The boys grew quickly, every day they seemed to stretch a little bit more, and their individual personalities started to develop. The black puppy was bigger and seemed more confident than his shy, timid brother, who was extremely cuddly and affectionate. It's always such an honour and a delight to watch them change from helpless, hamster-sized babies that I could hold in the palm of my hand, into proper playful puppies. After another few days, they started licking my hands and had grown a full set of baby teeth so the next task was weaning. Usually a messy business, these two took to it immediately and dived into a soupy porridge of soaked puppy biscuits and their special puppy milk. Their little faces emerged with milky beards before falling into a milk coma, and then straight off to sleep. I started to get a bit more sleep too, no longer setting the alarm for 5 am, I could lie in until 6.30. Luxury.

They started to make rapid progress, every day saw tiny changes and by four weeks old they recognised me and squealed with excitement at every mealtime. After each feed, they played with toys and shook the edges of their blankets fiercely, or jumped on each other with their newfound barks and growls.

Their energy only lasted ten or fifteen minutes before they curled up together, circling round and round, establishing who would be cuddler and who would be cuddlee, then, as if a switch had been turned off, they were asleep. I loved watching them for a few minutes, as their legs twitched and their mouths sucked at the air, as if at a teat. Puppies are surprisingly active and vocal in sleep, I could only wonder what they were dreaming about.

Another week passed and as they grew heavier and more wriggly, I knew the time was coming for them to move on. They needed to have some freedom to run and play and I can no longer get down onto the floor with them, or pick them up. My spinal fusion meant that I couldn't bend or twist or reach for them, now they were more active and unpredictable. I called Filipa and we made a plan.

The other two puppies were being fostered by another of her clients, who had set up a puppy playroom for them. It made sense for my two to join them for this important part of their puppyhood, learning to be a dog. From around five weeks they start to play fight and learn bite inhibition as their siblings will cry and pull away if they are too rough. This socialisation is vital, even at such an early age, in setting down the groundwork for a happy and confident adult dog.

Fiona rang and we chatted about the pups, she was obviously doing a great job with her two and agreed it was time for mine to be reunited with their brother and sister.

On their last day with me, we had extra cuddles, and I shed a few tears. Little did they know that their little lives were about to change completely. I heard the car draw up and placed them back into their cage for the last time.

It's always sad to see them go, but I've done my bit and it's time for them to move on to the next stage. For now, I can only wish them long and happy lives as I dismantle the cage and wash the last load of blankets, ready for next time. All the pups were re-homed locally, and are doing well.

The black puppy (Lucky) with his new big brother

23

After back surgery, life in paradise

To my surprise, I received a lot of comments and questions about my surgery since my previous book, *Another Day in Paradise* was published. I actually didn't plan to include it at all but had written my account of my surgery shortly after the event, mainly to keep a record for myself. However, I was persuaded to use it, and I am glad now that I did.

I didn't want to focus on the negatives, I prefer to talk about the people we meet, the amusing incidents and the kindness of strangers, rather than a doom and gloom account of disability, but as I have been asked, here are some of the things I deal with on a day-to-day basis.

My spine is fixed with titanium rods and screws, from roughly bra-strap level, right to the bottom (T10-L5 vertebrae). There is no bending or flexing, twisting or turning, at all. As the vertebrae are all fused together, there is no cushioning, no shock absorbers.

I know it is difficult to imagine that I can't sit down. It's such a normal thing, chairs are everywhere, 'Are you sitting comfortably?' 'Let's have a nice sit-down.' For me, you could remove all the chairs, sofas and stools in the world, and I wouldn't notice. When I first started venturing out to cafes and restaurants post-op, we were governed by what kind of seats they had. I take two cushions everywhere now, one orthopaedic, a spinal cushion to sit on, and another to put behind me. Even with these, I am still uncomfortable, but I can put up with it for a short time. A chair that's too low, or too high, or too slippery, or without arms all add to the problem. I need to be upright, but not too upright. Just at the right angle so that my shoulders take more weight than my spine. Once I'm seated, I can't lean forward, so everything has to be within arm's length. I can't eat spaghetti or soup in a restaurant as they will just drip all over me as I transfer from plate to mouth. There have been times when I just have to stand up and walk around a bit, or even abandon our plans and come home due to the pain.

The only time I'm at ease is when lying flat - and flat has to mean completely flat. I can feel if there's a slight wrinkle in a sheet, which is ironic as I used to love reading 'The Princess and the Pea' as a child, where the queen puts a pea under a girl's mattress and if she feels it, the queen will deem her sensitive enough to marry her son, the Prince!

I need my cushions in the car too and the seat has to be at the correct angle. Recently I managed to put one of my back cushions in upside down. I thought I'd be able to manage for the ten minutes or so until we stopped, but had to get Nick to pull over halfway. That slight misalignment meant I was almost in tears and feeling nauseous.

I now have one leg shorter than the other, since my spine has been straightened out. At home I wear one flip-flop on the short leg, to balance me up, otherwise, I start the day already at a disadvantage in the pain department. I get some strange looks from couriers and tradespeople. Some will actually ask,

"Do you know you only have one flip-flop on?" or "Have you lost a shoe?" As if I didn't already know I was just wearing one.

I used to take my shoes to a German guy who had a similar problem, following a skiing accident. He would very cleverly build up the sole of one shoe, matching the material and colour exactly, so it was difficult to see the extra height. Unfortunately, he moved back to Germany several years ago. Now I just have to put up with it when I'm out, but it does make walking any distance quite painful and tiring.

My hips and pelvis are also fixed, so I walk purely with my legs. I know that sounds a bit strange, we all walk with our legs, but I have no input from the rest of my body. I don't have the up and down rotation in the hips that gives purpose and momentum. I can't walk on unstable surfaces like grass and sand, or walk up or downhill, which is quite a problem living somewhere like Carvoeiro which is virtually all hills. I have to keep my legs and feet as level as possible and be aware of any potholes or dips in the pavement as my body can't compensate for them.

So, I can't sit, and can only walk short distances, but I also can't stand still. As anyone who knows me will recognise, if I have to stand I do so by constantly shifting my weight from side to side. No wonder I'm 80-90% housebound it's all just such a palaver.

I have 'grabbers' everywhere, which are very useful for picking up most things. Anything heavy or awkward, however, has to wait until Nick is around. If I have to get down to floor level, I kneel on one knee and push myself back up with the other leg. Consequently, my knees are beginning to complain and I can't face having to have any surgery on them, so I limit my kneeling as much as possible.

I can't swim normally now, but I do use a flotation belt to

exercise every day through the warmer months. I perform my own solo, synchronised swimming routines to a playlist of fast and slow music, using Pilates' techniques. Amazingly, I'm almost always synchronised with myself.

One of the most frequent comments, the first time someone saw me post-op was "But you look so well!" I'm not sure what they were expecting, but I'm still me, still the same person. I have a mechanical issue with my spine, but everything else is the same. I think I have retained the same, slightly dark, sense of humour, and I have the same interests as before.

I have tried to concentrate on what I can do, rather than what I've lost. I've taken up crochet again after being taught by my Nan as a child, and I have become rather addicted. Most people I know have acquired quite a selection of crocheted blankets, hats, and hand warmers. To save them from gifts of crochet bikinis or trouser suits, I decided to put my obsession to good use and make items to donate to the homeless, or families in need. I used to do a lot for a charity called Woolly Hugs in the UK but issues with customs and transport, post-Brexit, have meant it's no longer viable. I haven't found an EU supplier for the particular yarn they use, and sending parcels to the U.K. is now a costly, bureaucratic nightmare. It's such a shame as I really enjoyed making and sending squares or whole blankets to them and they do such good work.

We had to change my car, from a fairly low-slung hatchback to something with more headroom. I have to be able to get into a car without bending, so I'm unable to get into most standard cars. The first post-op vehicle we bought was a Hyundai Matrix, and I would have bought another one if they hadn't stopped making them a couple of years later. When it was on its last legs, I started researching for an alternative and narrowed it down to three or four options. Nick had previously bought a van from a local Ford dealership, so we went to test drive the Ecosport model. It looked quite chunky and had the necessary height, however, when I tried to get in it, I found it just wasn't practical for me. I was so disappointed. The salesman, Pedro, pointed to a dull, dark blue van-like lump in the car park.

"I have sold quite a few of those to people with back problems," he said, hopefully.

I stared at it, completely underwhelmed, still holding the keys to the shiny gold Ecosport.

"Do you want to try it?"

"No, I don't think so, it's not really what I had in mind."

"Just sit in it, it's very comfortable."

Reluctantly, I surrendered the keys and followed him. Pedro opened the door with a flourish,

"It has lots of space inside, you can adjust the seat in all directions, and the steering wheel. I slid into the driver's seat, I hated to admit just how easily. It had a huge windscreen and great all-round visibility. It just wasn't very attractive. Nick was opening the boot,

"Come and look at this, it's so spacious for its size, and there's no lip on here so it would make it much easier to load and unload." He was sounding more and more enthusiastic. "Oh, and the back doors slide, that's handy if you're in a tight parking space."

He and Pedro were deep in conversation now, each of them pointing out a new advantage. I got out and went to see what all the fuss was about. Pedro could feel a sale about to slip through his fingers.

"What don't you like about it?"

"The shape, the colour..."

His attention was taken by a car driving into the lot.

"Look, see that white car that just drove in?"

I nodded.

"This is the basic model, but that is the upgraded version, the Titanium, I think you will like it."

We crossed the car park again, and he called out to a colleague, who threw some keys to him.

"Let's go."

So off we went.

As we got closer, I had to admit that this model was a definite improvement. It was a brilliant white, with tinted rear windows and totally different styling. It was also about 5K cheaper than the Ecosport. Nick was sold, and I was coming round to the idea.

"We have one identical in stock in Lisbon, we can deliver it next week."

Pedro was optimistic about a sale again. They went off to negotiate a part-exchange price on the Hyundai while I acquainted myself with my new car, and tried to ignore the Ecosport, sulking in the corner. I grew to love the Tourneo, and when another new improved version came out three years later, we upgraded too. It really is a very comfortable and practical car, and extremely economical with just a 1000 cc engine but still smooth and responsive to drive. Thank you, Pedro.

Another consideration is taxis. The most common make here is a Mercedes saloon, but it is just no good for me. I decided to book a seven-seater people carrier for six of us (Nick and I, my parents, and Anne-Marie and Steve) to go out to celebrate my birthday. I hadn't explained my situation but just assumed it would have the necessary height. What I hadn't taken into account was that you step up into this type of vehicle.

When it arrived, it became clear that the actual height inside was not much different to a normal car. The restaurant was booked and there was no time to source an alternative, so I had to go with it. I ended up sliding into it on my knees, like a bad Toulouse-Lautrec impersonation, then pushing myself up onto the seat. Getting out at our destination proved even more difficult. I slid onto my knees then had to swivel around and reverse out of the door. The driver had come round to help us out and stared in disbelief at my antics, and this was before any drink had been taken. Apart from the trip to take my language exam in Faro, I haven't been in a taxi since.

I haven't been on a plane since 2008, and I can't foresee a time when I'll fly anywhere again. I couldn't have the seat upright enough for take-off and landing, never mind all the waiting around at the airport. Also, there's no way of testing it out; once airborne, I couldn't change my mind if it turned out to be too painful. I have missed weddings, birthdays and funerals, and our last foreign holiday was in 2006.

I now have a 'zero-gravity' wheelchair. It can be set to the correct angle for me, and also allows me to lie almost flat, if necessary, with leg and foot supports. It is useful if we're going anywhere that is likely to involve a long queue such as government departments and agencies. I have also used it in some restaurants, confusing people who see me walk in, then settle myself in the chair, but it is so much more comfortable than a normal seat.

I have an electric bed in the living room, and a garden bed, and if I'm not in our proper bed, I'm generally in one of the others. I watch TV, crochet and eat from my electric bed, as I can raise and lower the head and feet parts as required. I can't do such simple things as bend over the washbasin to brush my teeth and I am terrified of being sick and choking, as I can't kneel or bend over the loo. I can't put on socks or tights or wear shoes or boots with zips, buckles or laces. I can't cut or paint my own toenails. It can take several attempts to get dressed each morning, knickers and trousers are the worst so in summer I wear dresses every day.

When one of you is functioning at fifty per cent capacity and something happens to the other, the first person doesn't magically get better. Nick has had some health issues over the last few months, which have made life difficult, but thankfully we had lots of offers of help and we got through it.

Nearly twenty years after we locked up and left Crowthorne in England for the last time, and nearly thirty-five years since we first saw Carvoeiro, we are still here. We have seen lots of people come and go in that time. It is easy to see why they come, but there are three main reasons why they leave: health, family, financial. We have had excellent care from both the private and state health service, but it can be scary to negotiate and some people prefer to be treated on home ground.

For others, it's the pull of family, especially children and grandchildren when they come along, and finally, some just can't make a go of it here. It is difficult, salaries are still low, although the minimum wage is increasing and now stands at

750€ per month, roughly double what it was when we arrived. Running a business is fraught with red-tape and if it's not going to be seasonal and reliant on the tourist trade, then you need a good standard of Portuguese to succeed.

We have been incredibly lucky. We have worked hard and taken chances, but we have also been given opportunities, and we are extremely grateful to everyone who has helped us along the way. It can cause conflict when one partner wants to stay and the other is desperate to leave, we have seen that too, but we have both been on the same page throughout.

We are often asked what we miss from the UK. My first two answers are an airing cupboard, and coming here on holiday. I've got used to the first one now, but living here just isn't the same as being on holiday; we don't do the same things now, maybe we should. I do miss M&S-style ready meals, as an occasional treat. There isn't much of a 'ready meal culture' here apart from frozen pizza and lasagne, but I do a lot of batch cooking for the freezer so I guess it's healthier this way.

As with *Another Day in Paradise,* I have written this book on my phone. It's tough with such a small screen and having to scroll back and forwards as I write, but it's the only way for me to do it comfortably.

We are still looking after our street cats. Ella has recently started running to meet me, it has only taken her three years to get used to me. She has recently been joined by two or three others, one of whom I'm sure has a home and is just being cheeky. One has a clipped ear, so is spayed, but there are two that haven't so we will be borrowing Cliff and Sue's trap again, once Nick is back to full fitness.

We are approaching the next phase of our lives, slowing

down and taking things a bit easier. Nick is no longer doing 12-hour days, 6 days a week, but I don't see him fully retiring just yet. He enjoys what he does, being out and about, meeting and helping people, and will continue to do so as long as he's able.

We are still enjoying our little piece of Paradise.

———————

Also by Karen Telling

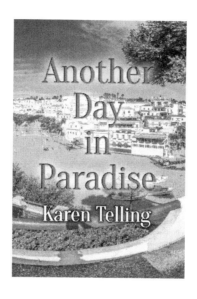

"Written by a remarkable woman, an overcomer, an inspiration."

"I loved this. An honest and insightful read into starting over."

"Moving, amusing, and a wonderful love letter to Portugal."

"Beautifully written book, especially if you know and love Carvoeiro."

"So refreshing to find a book like this, reminds me of Driving Over Lemons but with some very comic pets who threaten to steal the show with their antics. Wonderfully written."

Acknowledgements

I would like to thank everyone who has agreed, or even volunteered, to let me tell your part in our story. It would have been a far less interesting journey without you. There are many others too, but I am very aware of their right to privacy, especially if they're not native English speakers and therefore unable to read the book.

Thank you to my cheerleaders and beta readers once again, Ellen, Anne-Marie and Rhona.

We are always grateful to Dra Filipa Costa, our vet, friend, and my 'Portuguese sister', and her colleagues for their help, support and advice.

Thank you also to the local businesses who have supported me since the publication of *Another Day in Paradise* -

The Algarve Book Cellar
Earth Café
The Soares Family at Cepsa,
Rocha Brava Reception
CultnArt Café
The Bed Warehouse,
Direct Transport,
Lara Haylee Costa
Roosters

and local publications - The Portugal News
The Resident
Tomorrow Magazine

I am extremely grateful to Caroline Mylon for her endless support and encouragement in editing this book, to Karolina Robinson for creating another cover for me, and to Keith Abbott at Michael Terence Publishing for pulling all the strands together.

For Nick, for his continued love and support over the last 37 years, even though there has been more 'in sickness' than 'in health'.

We continue to support a number of charities in the Algarve, for more information please check the following Facebook pages -

Algarve Network for Families in Need
Associação Alerta de Incêndio Florestal/Forestfire Alert
Benafim Dogs
Mayday Algarve
Goldra Dog Sanctuary
Tiny Shelter, Albufeira
Friends of Portimão Canil
AEZA
Lar Crianças Bom Samaritano (Children's Home)
Carvoeiro Cat Charity

Finally, we owe a big thank you to all the people who have helped us along this journey, far too many to mention, but I think you all know who you are.

To keep up-to-date with life in Carvoeiro…
and for a photo album to accompany this book please go to
www.facebook.com/karentellingwriter
or scan the QR code below

If you have enjoyed *Our Little Piece of Paradise*
or *Another Day in Paradise…*
I would be grateful if you could leave a rating or review on
Amazon or Goodreads, thank you.
Scan the QR code below for my Amazon Author page

Printed in Great Britain
by Amazon